I Am Curious (Yellow)

"*I Am Curious* accuses, with amazing poisonousness, monarchy, Social Democracy, neutrality, and the Swedish standard of living; that is, the main supports of Scandinavia's good conscience . . . *I Am Curious* is not just a film made by a moralist, it is also a film by a great cinéast." —Pierre Billard, *L'Express* (Paris)

"His ferocity is despair: Sjöman pulls down all the barriers he discovers, including the outermost sex barrier. But the prison remains: the stronghold of Puritanism, nationalism, egocentricity."
—Lasse Bergström, *Expressen* (Stockholm)

"A naked, desperate revolt against well-fed, self-congratulatory, hypocritical, blue-and-yellow-flag-waving Sweden . . ." —Finn Carling, *Dagbladet* (Oslo)

"Films for all times exist in large numbers, lying about moldering in the film archives and in our memories. Sjöman's film is an active political act right here and now in the Swedish arena, a thrust toward the heart of our lukewarmness and our neutrality."

—Mauritz Edström, *Dagens Nyheter* (Stockholm)

". . . *I Am Curious* marks an important date. With its release, all the 'allusive' films of the past seventy years, all those scenes of seduction which fade out chastely, have with one blow aged by twenty years. In several years, with the exception of the *chef d'oeuvres*, the majority among them will seem hypocritical and ridiculous. They will be appreciated for their 'camp' side, like comics and cloche hats."

—Michel Mardore, *Nouvel Observateur* (Paris)

I Am Curious (Yellow)

A film by Vilgot Sjöman

Translated from the Swedish
by Martin Minow and Jenny Bohman

Grove Press, Inc., New York

Library of Congress Catalog Card Number: 68-54005
Fifth printing
An Evergreen Black Cat Book
Manufactured in the United States of America

Contents

1. The elevator

Someone is overheard composing a jingle, "At Sandrews they make good films . . ." A well-dressed elderly woman enters the building at Kungsgatan 65, Stockholm. Unfortunately, the elevator is already occupied by a burly middle-aged man and a pint-sized young woman who's pulling at his tie ingratiatingly. They are LENA NYMAN, DRAMA STUDENT, AGE 22, *and* VILGOT SJÖMAN, YOUNG DIRECTOR, AGE 42*; who have just been visiting Sandrews, the film company. The elderly woman is disgusted.*

Over a close-up of Lena, the title:

I AM CURIOUS

Over a close-up of Vilgot:

I AM CURIOUS

LADY (*answering the titles*): But *I'm* not. You stick to your films!

Visibly annoyed, she turns her back and walks up the stairs to Saga, a sports organization located in the same building.

For a moment Lena is distressed.

LENA: Oh. I thought it was my old lady.

VILGOT: Your old lady?! Oooh!

2. Slogans

Dusk. A trade-union hall. Above the building flies the Swedish flag, a yellow cross on a blue background.

MALE VOICE: Buy our film. Buy it! Buy it! The only film that's shown in two editions: One yellow and one blue!

FEMALE VOICE: Buy the yellow! Buy the blue!
Buy our film because it's two!

MALE VOICE: Exactly the same picture, yet so different.

FEMALE VOICE: Big things and little things!

MALE VOICE: The blue picture!

FEMALE VOICE: Beautiful things and ugly things!

VOICES: The yellow picture! This is the yellow edition! Yes, the yellow edition! The yellow edition! Presenting the yellow edition! This is the yellow edition!

3. Yevtushenko reads poetry

A meeting hall inside the building. Yevgeny **YEVTUSHENKO, RUSSIAN POET, AGE 33,** *stands before a microphone at Clarté, a radical political organization. But the sound system doesn't work. There are catcalls.*

VOICES: Louder! Louder! Check the one to the right. No, no, the left. Further left. The left! (*Chanting:*) To the left, the left, the left. Further to the left.

Laughter. Lena and Vilgot are in the audience. Lena hums an old sailor's song.

LENA: "In Rio de Janeiro you can fuck for free . . ."

VILGOT (*embarrassed*): Quiet.

LENA: Look over there. Do you see that guy?

VILGOT: Yes.

LENA: Magnus. He's an actor at the University theater. He would be fine as the slave.

VILGOT: Him?

LENA: Mmm. And I could have a little love scene with him.

VILGOT: Oh, I see.

LENA: Hmm.

VILGOT: And what would that love scene be like?

LENA: Oh, just a quickie, you know.

VILGOT: Well . . .

Confusion on the stage. The microphone still doesn't work. No one can find out what's wrong. Yevtushenko loses his patience and speaks in a loud voice directly to the audience.

YEVTUSHENKO: Dear friends! I have heard that quite a few members of Clarté are revolutionary. But if they're

going to organize the revolution the way they've organized tonight's meeting—how will that end?

Laughter and applause. The reading soon begins.

VILGOT (*voice over*): It's a damn shame that Lena doesn't understand politics. But God, drama students!

Yevtushenko begins reading.

YEVTUSHENKO: "There are no memorials over Babi Yar.
Only an abrupt bank like a crude
epitaph rears . . ."

VILGOT (*voice over*): Well, one day I'll tell Lena about the fate of socialism in Sweden. No! I'll have to tell her about the two heads of Swedish socialism: the big self-satisfied head and the little shrunken one.

Photos of workingmen in the thirties; then shots of a mongoloid child beating his head against the metal bars of a crib.

4. Lena sleeps over

The same evening, after the reading, at Vilgot's apartment. Lena washes her face and crawls into bed with the outline for a film, LENA ON THE ROAD: A KALEIDOSCOPE. *Vilgot looks at photographs of ancient erotic Indian temple sculptures while he trims his hair with electric clippers and hums a song he is composing.*

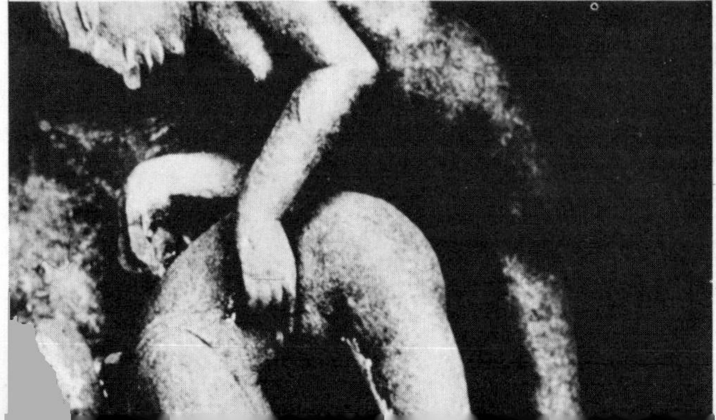

VILGOT (*sings*): "I like my own sweet name.
I like the touch of fame.
I like my own sweet name.
I like the touch of fame."

VILGOT (*voice over*): Sneak Lena into my bed. She doesn't even dare to tell her mother that she's spending the night with me. Oh, no, her mother is supposed to believe that Lena is staying with some girl friend from drama school.

Vilgot goes into the room. Lena pretends to be asleep. In Lena on the Road, *Lena will often wear different kinds of glasses, both old and new. Vilgot begins to try them on her. Sometimes she looks like a little child; sometimes like an old grandmother.*

It is dangerous to be in love with your star. So Ingmar Bergman used to tell me. "You become blind

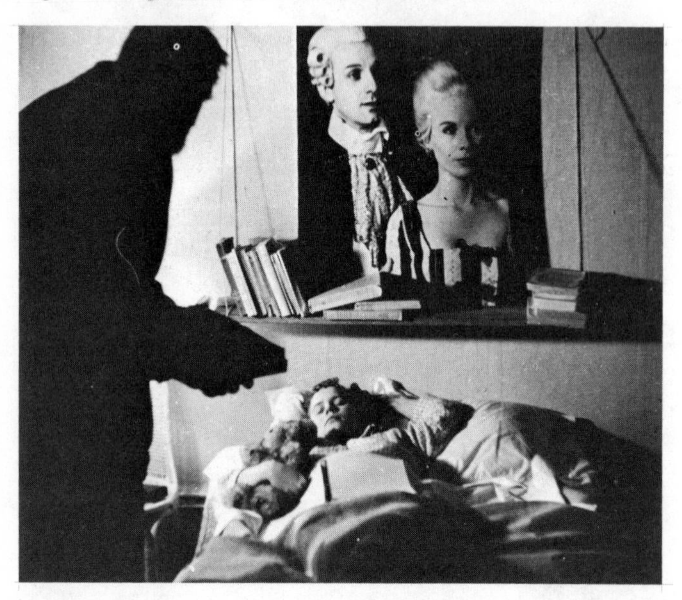

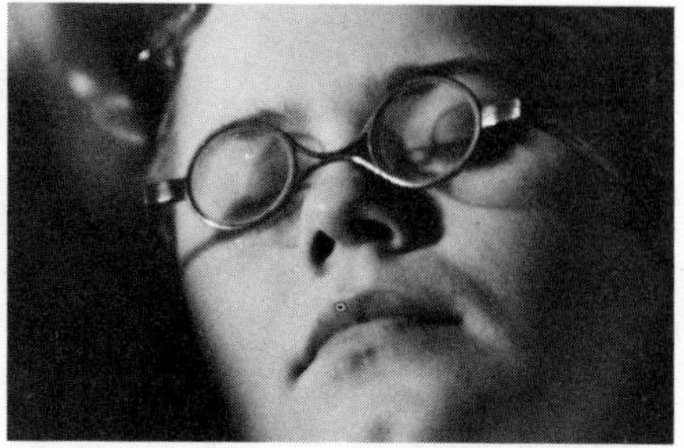

to her affectations," he said. It never happened to him, though.

I met Lena when we shot *491*, but nothing much happened then. We were a bit turned on to each other, that's all. . . . There've been some changes made.

Lena wakens from her make-believe sleep and grabs Vilgot by the beard, pulls him down to her.

VILGOT: Ouch!

5. *Lena asks questions*

Vilgot sends Lena into the streets of Stockholm to collect interview material for the new film. She is assisted by Ulla Lyttkens, another drama student, and Magnus, who is to play the slave.

Lena walks into a restaurant kitchen, carrying a tape recorder and microphone.

LENA: Do you think that Swedish society has a class system?

WOMAN IN RESTAURANT KITCHEN: Class system, how do you mean?

Ulla in an auto repair shop.

FOREMAN: Strictly speaking, I don't think it has. We have . . . I mean, everybody is kind of sticking together.

In a restaurant near the dock.

FIRST DOCK WORKER: I don't know. I can't answer that. Ask somebody else.

SECOND DOCK WORKER: I don't think it has.

LENA: You don't?

SECOND DOCK WORKER: No.

In a post office.

OLD MESSENGER: No politics for me, thanks!

Outside a shop. Lena is kneeling in the doorway.

LENA: Do you think that Swedish society has a class system?

THREE-YEAR-OLD BOY: Yes.

LENA: You do?

THREE-YEAR-OLD BOY: Yes.

Lena with two students, recently engaged.

LENA: An architect or a doctor earns ten to fifteen times more than a dishwasher. Do you think that's fair?

FEMALE STUDENT: Yes, I think that's fair.

MALE STUDENT: Sure, that's fair.

FEMALE STUDENT: When you consider that an education takes at least seven years and how much you have to deny yourself during that time . . .

Magnus is taking still photographs of some of the subjects.

In a restaurant.

LENA (*voice over*): But ten to fifteen times more! I think that's too much. Much too much!

YOUNG WORKER (*complacently*): Well . . . I don't think it's that bad.

In the street.

SALVATION ARMY OFFICER: It's fair to the extent that those who aren't clever enough can hardly go on with their studies. Studying is a thorny path and few people have the energy to do it. I have to go now.

In a repair shop.

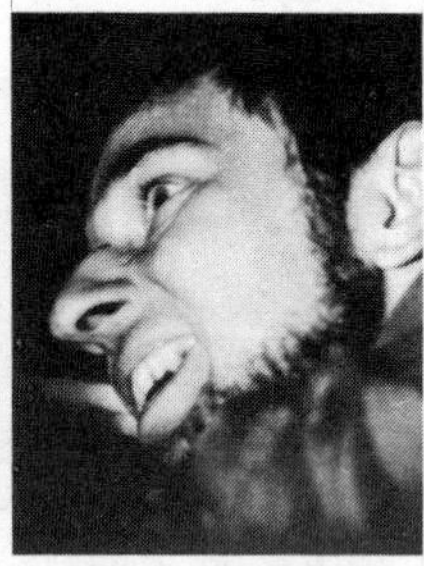

ULLA: Do you think that women have the same opportunities as men in our society?

MAN WITH "VOLVO" CAP: Yes, I suppose they have.

ANOTHER MECHANIC: Yes, sure they have, if not more. (*Smiling.*) Don't you think that the women are running things now?

In a hospital corridor, Lena approaches two young nurses' aides.

LENA: Do you think that there is a hierarchy in this hospital?

FIRST NURSES' AID (*shyly*): No.

LENA: So you don't think there is a difference between doctors and nurses' aids?

SECOND NURSES' AID: Of course, the time you eat is different.

LENA: The time you eat?

SECOND NURSES' AID: Yes, the time you eat.

In the subway.

ULLA: Do you think that Swedish society has a class system?

YOUNG MAN: What?

ULLA: Do you think that Swedish society has a class system?

YOUNG MAN: No.

ULLA: Can you explain yourself?

YOUNG MAN: I don't get what you're saying.

He hurries off. Ulla approaches a man walking, reading a newspaper.

ULLA: Excuse my interrupting your reading. Do you think Sweden has a class system?

MAN WITH NEWSPAPER: I am not Swedish.

ULLA: Don't you understand Swedish?

MAN WITH NEWSPAPER: I understand it. But I'm not Swedish.

LADY IN HAT: I don't understand. I am German.

UNSHAVEN MAN: I–I–am–not–Swedish.

ULLA: Do you think that Sweden has a class system?

MAN IN HAT: Yes.

MAN IN GLASSES: A what?

ULLA: A class system.

MAN IN GLASSES: Yes, in a way.

In a department store.

LADY IN FEATHER HAT: Yes, I think it has.

LADY IN GLASSES: No, I don't think so.

ULLA: So you think that Sweden has gone as far as it can in removing class barriers?

LADY IN GLASSES: Yes, it just might go a little bit farther, but . . .

BEARDED YOUNG MAN: I don't think you can go much farther as far as that's concerned. There has to be a difference in wages according to efficiency, so to speak, if society is to function.

In an elegant shoe store.

BOOTBLACK: Oh, this kind of interview I don't like . . .

In the subway.

MAN IN HAT AND COAT: In the thirties there was a difference between the classes. At that time we had the white-collar workers. The gap between the classes is just as wide today, if not wider.

In a restaurant kitchen.

CHEF: It depends on the people themselves, doesn't it? Undress them all! When they are naked they're all alike. Dress them again and you have the class system.

6. Lena at the Forbundshuset

LENA (*voice over*): In order to try to understand all this better I decided to go to the headquarters of the labor movement at Branting's Square.

Lena goes into the offices of the Carpenters' Union. In the corridor, she meets an ombudsman on his way to Parliament.

OMBUDSMAN: There couldn't be a class system. Don't we live in a democracy? In a democratic society?

Lena goes down to the cafeteria. Since people who don't work for trade unions also eat here, she has to ask her way along the cafeteria line.

LENA: Do you belong to the labor movement?
MAN: What now?
LENA: Are you with the labor movement?
MAN: No.
LENA: Is anybody?
MAN: No, not here.
LENA: Labor movement?
VOICE: No.
LENA: Are you with the labor movement?
ANOTHER VOICE: NO!

Lena finds two ombudsmen seated at a table.

LENA: Why is the labor movement so damned conservative when it comes to women's rights?
FIRST OMBUDSMAN: So you find the labor movement conservative on the subject of women's rights!

In the offices of The Metalworker.

EDITOR-IN-CHIEF: I guess that's partially true. But it could

* A building housing Sweden's major trade-union organizations.

possibly be partly due to the fact that we have a lot of conservatives in this country. And there's bound to be quite a few of them even in the labor movement.

In the cafeteria, with the ombudsmen.

LENA: But why is it that women have fewer chances of getting good jobs?
SECOND OMBUDSMAN: You're the one who's claiming that.
LENA: Sure, I'm the one who's claiming that. Do *you* claim that it isn't so?
SECOND OMBUDSMAN: No, I don't have to make any claims. You have to prove that you are right.
FIRST OMBUDSMAN: Yes, let's have some proof! You shouldn't go around making claims when you don't know the facts.
LENA: My mother works as a furrier. She works every day of the year. She makes about 14,000 kroner.*
SECOND OMBUDSMAN: But if I became a furrier, what would I get?
LENA: But you won't become a furrier.
SECOND OMBUDSMAN: You never know.

Lena finds an architect in the cafeteria.

LENA: Do you think that Swedish society has a class system?
ARCHITECT: Well, I think it has—to a certain extent.
LENA: What are you going to do about it?
ARCHITECT (*smiling*): I'm going to climb up the ladder. You've got to live in the society you were born into.
LENA: Do you work for the labor movement?
ARCHITECT: No, I don't.
LENA: What do you do then?
ARCHITECT: I'm an architect.

* One dollar equals approximately 5.18 kroner.—*Trans.*

Lena, with the two ombudsmen again.

FIRST OMBUDSMAN: Oh, yes, there is a class system, of course there is.

LENA: What are you going to do about it?

SECOND OMBUDSMAN: We aren't going to do anything about it, at least not for the moment.

LENA: Why not?

SECOND OMBUDSMAN: Since we all live in a society with class barriers, I'm a part of it. And then, you know, there are democratic rules, and the individual doesn't have a direct influence on development.

In an office.

SECRETARY: I'm sure the individual can't do very much.
LENA (*voice over*): Nothing? Can't he do anything?
SECRETARY: No, I don't think so.

In a corridor.

LADY WITH UPSWEPT HAIR: I'm not an active union member.

In the cafeteria.

MAN'S VOICE: But we're going to negotiate.
LENA: Negotiate?

MAN'S VOICE: Yes.
LENA: What will happen then?
MAN'S VOICE: You don't know?
LENA: No, I don't.
MAN'S VOICE: Don't you keep up with things like that?
LENA: No.
MAN'S VOICE: And yet you run around asking questions.
LENA: So I've got to ask you people who do know.

MAN'S VOICE: Then read the newspapers. You can learn a lot from them.

LENA: You can't tell me? What happens at those negotiations? Are there any results? How long will it take before the class barriers can be removed? Equal wages and no class system!

A MAN: A very long time, probably.

LENA: Why?

THE MAN: Because people are conservative. They don't want any radical changes.

LENA: Like what, for example?

ANOTHER MAN: Extended government programs, for example . . . Increased participation in management decisions, that's another thing . . .

LENA: Anything else?

THE OTHER MAN (*to a friend across from him*): Well, what else are we going to do?

In the offices of The Metalworker.

LENA: You really think that you are doing something to get rid of the class system?

EDITOR: As much as I can.

LENA: Can't you do anything more?

EDITOR: It all has to do with what position you have in society.

LENA: Do you have to be at the very top in order to do anything at all?

EDITOR: No, no, no! This is a matter of applying pressure from underneath that will have an effect all the way up.

LENA: But the real big-shots who have influence and power to do a lot—do they use it?

7. At the home of Olof Palme

The question leads directly to **OLOF PALME, AGE 39,** *then* **MINISTER OF TRANSPORT** *in the Social-Democratic government. In foreign affairs he is known for his sharp criticism of the American role in the Vietnam war. On domestic issues, he has been called "a fanatic about equality."*

OLOF PALME: In many ways we still have some of the characteristics of the old class system. We have, as I think someone has said, a class system by income, and you can see exactly why.

Rural workers have lower wages than urban workers. Women earn less than men, and older people less than the young. Education perpetuates the class system. University graduates get six to seven times more than those who leave school and go straight to work in the country.

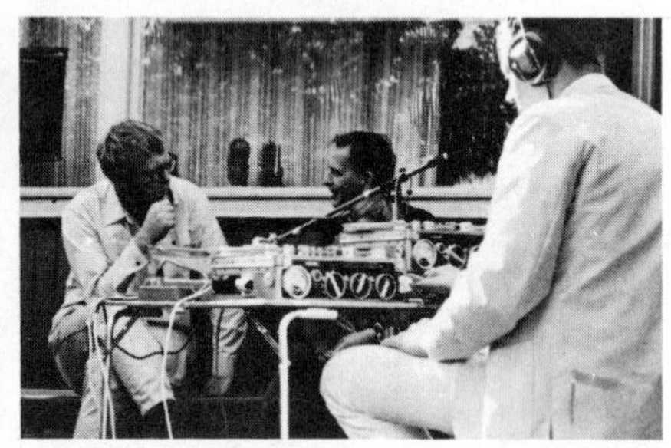

Olof Palme lives in a little row house outside Stockholm. The film crew is working in the backyard. Magnus happens to be present. He is sitting beside Lena, which irritates Vilgot. The filming is also interrupted by **MÅRTEN (MOUSIE), AGE 5,** *who is banging against the wall from inside the house.*

VILGOT (*breaking off*): Come outside, Mousie! You see, if

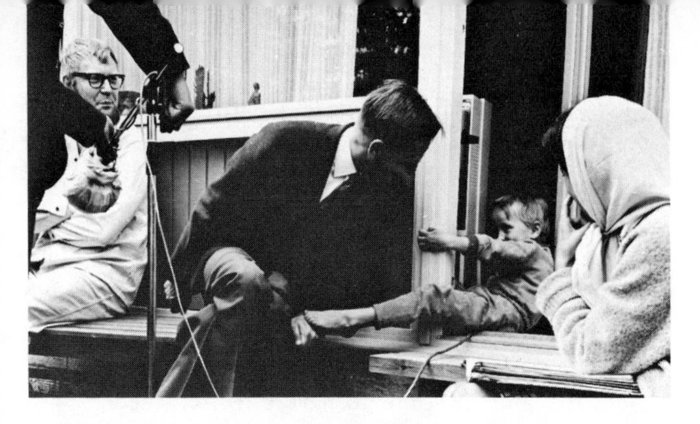

you make that noise, it'll ruin the sound track.

The shooting has stopped. The boy crawls up onto Palme's knee. The cameramen load the camera. Vilgot asks Palme how he became a Social Democrat.

OLOF PALME: Well, this problem of class system in Swedish society—I feel very strongly about it. That's what I've reacted against from the beginning . . .

VILGOT: What is your own background?

OLOF PALME: I come from a middle-class family. You learn a lot through books, you observe a lot, and suddenly it starts forming a pattern. This happened to me sometime between the ages of fifteen and twenty—around the time when I saw American society.

VILGOT: You traveled in the States? About what year was that?

OLOF PALME: '47 to '48. I hitchhiked.

VILGOT: I see.

OLOF PALME: Thirty-four states. Three months without money.

VILGOT: I see.

OLOF PALME: You see, it's mixed up with the books you read. You read fiction: I think that some fiction has enormous political importance. For me, in any case.

VILGOT: I see.

OLOF PALME: This—in connection with political theory and visual impressions—that's quite a rough combination.

The filming drags on. Palme's wife, Lisbeth, looks out from an upstairs window and wonders how much more time the crew will need. Mousie jumps around on his father's knee and waves to his mother.

LISBETH PALME: Mousie was going to ask you a few questions too. But he seems to have forgotten them.
VILGOT: I see. Do you have any questions, Mousie?
LISBETH PALME: He didn't think there was any point in Olof's becoming an M.P.
OLOF PALMES (*smiles*): That's a good thought in itself.

The camera is loaded. The shooting resumes.

VILGOT: Well, take Sweden from this point of view:

Foreigners tend to think that we are very far ahead. Do you think we are?

OLOF PALME: Yes, somewhat. I mean, we're far ahead compared to other countries. And we're far ahead compared to what Sweden looked like thirty to forty years ago. But we have *not* gone very far if you want your dream of a classless society to come true. In that case, most of the work remains to be done!

Vilgot finds it difficult to concentrate. To tease him, Lena moves even closer to Magnus, looking at Vilgot with a big grin.

8. The cutting room

In order to be alone, Vilgot goes up to his cutting room at Sandrews. Evening. Silent and peaceful.

VILGOT (*voice over*): Isn't it sad that—in spite of a Social-Democratic government for thirty years—so little has been done?

Lena surprises him! She sneaks in and puts her hands on his shoulders. He becomes irritated.

VILGOT: No, not now!

LENA: Are you angry? (*Looks at him.*) Oh yes, you are angry!

Lena looks at a death notice taped to the editing table.

†

VILGOT SJÖMAN

BORN DECEMBER 2, 1924

DIED JUNE 9, 1974

THE FUNERAL HAS TAKEN PLACE

LENA: 1974? That's six or seven years from now! So you've decided to live that long?

VILGOT: Stop playing games, will you?

LENA: You *are* in a bad mood!

VILGOT: Hell yes! The way you and Magnus acted at Palme's!

LENA: What's this?

VILGOT: I really need some peace and quiet to be able to make this picture. Now if you sit there and—even if you're not doing anything—I just can't work.

LENA: Oh, I can't stand listening to Palme. I don't get what the hell he's talking about.

VILGOT: You could at least pretend, couldn't you? Now that we're making this picture, you could at least pretend to understand what it's all about.

LENA: Is that why you won't let me have a love scene with Magnus? Don't you want a girl for the lead?

VILGOT: Yes, I do.

LENA: And you want a girl in bed too?

VILGOT: Yes.

LENA: And if you manage to combine the two, that's just fine, eh?

VILGOT: So what? Don't you want the lead?

LENA: Yes.

VILGOT: And don't you want somebody in bed as well?

LENA: Yes.

VILGOT: So who's using whom?

LENA: We're using each other. But don't go and say it's on the same terms. Don't say that!

Vilgot cannot find any answer. He smiles and turns to the editing table. He begins to run a previously filmed interview for Lena.

This was made in March, 1966, when **MARTIN LUTHER KING, JR., AGE 37,** *was in Stockholm with Harry Belafonte to initiate a large Swedish fund-raising*

campaign for American Negroes. After a speech to students at Stockholm University, he took the time to answer some questions on non-violence.

VILGOT: Do you have to have a religious belief to take part in a non-violent movement?

MARTIN LUTHER KING: No, not necessarily.

VILGOT: If you find that a person cannot stand being attacked, what do you do with him? Do you speak to him and explain to him that he cannot be with you any longer?

MARTIN LUTHER KING: Well, we always discourage those who cannot be subjected to attack—the one who would retaliate with violence—*not* to participate in a demonstration. The rules are very rigid in a non-violent movement and we feel that a person who can't take it—a person who cannot submit himself to violence if it comes to him and who would retaliate with violence—should not at all participate and so we discourage that person completely.

Lena seems fascinated by King.

LENA: I like him. He talks about better things than Palme.

Vilgot grimaces at the childish comment. But it gives him something to think about. In the forthcoming film, he wants to present Lena with three idols: a Russian, an American, and a Swede, to whom Lena turns for imaginary interviews when she is confused and depressed. Yevtushenko could be her Russian idol; Palme, her Swedish; and Martin Luther King, Jr., her American, because he represents the dream of non-violence. Non-violence should be another theme in the film, in contrast to the Swedish class system.

9. "If Sweden were occupied?"

Vilgot sends Lena and Ulla out to investigate what the general public knows about non-violence.

MAN IN GLASSES: Non-violence?
MAN: Non-violence?
MAN IN HAT: Non-violence?
ANOTHER MAN: Non-violence?
MAN IN COAT: Well, those hippies—aren't they involved in something like that?

Ulla asks two policemen on patrol.

ULLA: Have you ever heard of non-violence?
FIRST POLICEMAN: Non-violence?
ULLA: Yes.
FIRST POLICEMAN: No, I haven't.
SECOND POLICEMAN: No, I've never heard of it.

ULLA: Thank you.

Ulla asks a dock worker.

DOCK WORKER: Those who don't use violence? Well, I guess those are educated people who don't want to hurt others.

LADY IN BERET: Dr. Martin Luther King, for example.

ULLA: That's right. Do you know what methods he uses?

LADY IN CLOCHE HAT: Yes, he doesn't want to fight for his ideas.

Lena walks into an induction center. Boys eighteen and nineteen years old have to pass a physical examination before they are assigned to the Army, Navy, or Air Force—young boys ready for slaughter if Sweden is drawn into a war.

LENA: Have you ever thought of becoming a conscientious objector?

VOICE: No, I haven't.

SITTING BOY: No, never.

BOY AT THE WALL: No.

BARE-CHESTED BOY: No.

BOY WEARING CHAIN: No.

BOY IN TURTLE-NECK SWEATER: Oh yes, I have.

BLOND BOY: Like many others, I guess, I want to get out

as soon as possible. And it seems it would be sooner if I don't resist.

BOY IN SWEATER: You only have to serve longer if you refuse to bear arms.

A hot discussion is going on outside the induction center. A group of Provies is passing out handbills. They are explaining to another young man that there are loopholes in the new Swedish draft laws. One leaflet reads:* **YOU ARE FREE FROM MILITARY DUTY, IF YOU . . .**

A boy in uniform laughs at the young idealists.

---

* From "provacateur." Originally a group of young people in Holland with leftist tendencies whose program was essentially anti-authoritarian and anarchistic. There are now groups of Provos all over Europe. In Sweden, they are called "Provies"—"pro"-for; "vie"-life.—*Trans.*

BOY IN UNIFORM: Yes, but the military pays me for ten months, and I get to be here in Stockholm. I have room and board and a great time. I'm through by 1:30 and then I can go down . . .

PROVO (*voice over*): And what's more important, you get to learn how to kill.

ANOTHER PROVO (*voice over*): You are part of a system, you know, and its main mission is killing.

A VOICE: We are part of a system of violence.

Lena appears, takes a handbill, and soon enters into the discussion.

BOY IN FUR COLLAR: We have no pat alternative to how to act in a war, but . . .

LENA: So you think we should keep our defense?

BOY IN FUR COLLAR: Absolutely not.
LENA: Why not refuse absolutely?
BOY IN FUR COLLAR: Sure, you should absolutely refuse military service. What you shouldn't refuse, though, is to work for peace with some civilian institution.
BOY IN CAP: There are alternative services. We encourage everyone to refuse to do *military* service.

Inside the induction center.

LENA: If Sweden were occupied, how do you think we should defend ourselves then? Do you think there is any way of continuing to fight?
BOY IN UNIFORM: But I have already explained that I'm not trained for combat, so they don't teach me things like that.
LENA: Do they teach it to those who are?
BOY IN UNIFORM: Probably. Ask them.
BOY IN SUIT: I don't know. I don't think so.
SHIRTLESS BOY: It depends on what rank you are in the military.
LENA: And what would you others do, if we were invaded?
ANOTHER BOY IN UNIFORM: You know, like, one should never surrender. Sweden won't give up. And all those radio messages and that kind of talk about Sweden being defeated, that's just nonsense and we shouldn't worry about it.
LENA: Is that what you're taught?
BOY IN UNIFORM: That's kind of number one on the program. It's in this "If the war comes"—the pamphlet that's distributed to everybody.

Lena gets very upset when she realizes how little the military knows about non-violence. She brings Ulla and Magnus along and goes out to demonstrate in the streets of Stockholm. They carry posters reading:

REFUSE TO KILL
REFUSE MILITARY SERVICE
LET NON-VIOLENCE BE YOUR DEFENSE

10. Lena opens an Institute

Lena and Ulla work on a pamphlet, IF WE ARE OCCUPIED, *in which they argue that Sweden ought to have a non-violent defense system. Lena teaches Ulla the first argument.*

LENA: If you can teach a whole country, all its inhabitants, then they have a much better chance this way!

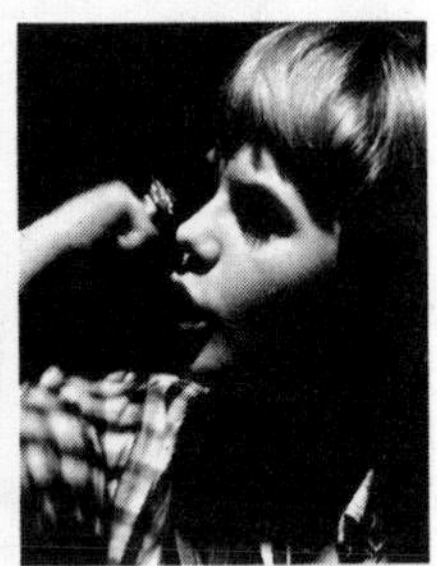

They must learn that many of them will die, that lots of them will be tortured—but what's good about it is that *less* people will die in this war than in a war where everybody keeps throwing bombs at each other. Thus you can reduce the number of dead. And that must be worth a hell of a lot.

Where were we now?

She holds up a cloth on which she has lettered in outline:

THE GUILTY CONSCIENCE OF SOCIAL DEMOCRACY

ULLA: We have: Negotiation. Mediation. Demonstrations. Sit-ins. Lie-ins. Strikes. Counter-demonstrations. Hunger strikes. Sabotage. Economic and social boycotts. Tax refusal. Civil disobedience. Paralysis of the entire society.

Even more methods can be invented. However, the basic ideas of a non-violent defense system can be summed up in these three slogans, which are flashed on the screen:

NON-COOPERATION
SABOTAGE
FRATERNIZATION

LENA: "Underground government," is that on your list as well?

ULLA: Yes, I've got that too.

To whom are we going to send this pamphlet?

LENA: To the Swedish Commander-in-Chief. They must be out of their minds not teaching us things like that!

Lena and Ulla also discuss different methods of masturbation.

LENA: I tried the shower hose yesterday.
ULLA: Did you?
LENA: Mmm.
ULLA: How was it?
LENA: It didn't work at all.
ULLA: Did you hold it the right way?
LENA: I held it the way you said. Like this.
ULLA: How about the vacuum cleaner? I know a girl who always uses the vacuum cleaner.
LENA: No, I'd rather use a massage machine.

Magnus arrives; he pauses before a new sign by the door, NYMAN'S INSTITUTE. *He brings a tape recorder and a typewriter that he bought on the black market. The girls are delighted. Magnus is afraid that Lena's father, snoring on the couch in the kitchen, will wake up.*

MAGNUS: Sssh!
LENA: Oh, don't worry. He's asleep. Hey, Dad, there's a civil war in Spain! Listen, riots in Adalen, they're shooting down workers! . . . General strike!

Her father continues snoring.

Well, what did I tell you?

Lena has opened an "Institute." Magnus asks her what her plans are.

Well, you have to start on your own, see. *They* don't do anything. The newspapers work far too fast, so they can't be trusted. And science works far too slowly, so you can't expect to get any results there. You've got to start on your own.

Hey, Magnus, will you start with the stencils?
MAGNUS (*picking up the empty black bag*): Lena, what's this bag?

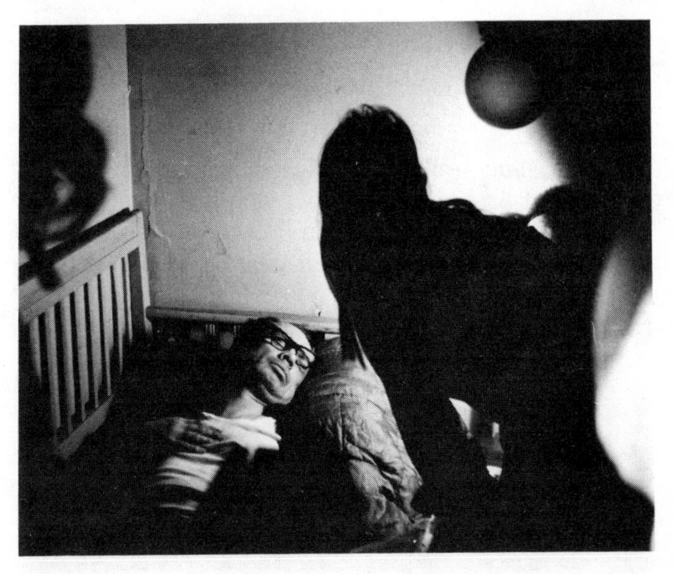

Lena has had a bright idea. The Social Democrats have been in power in Sweden for thirty years. In spite of that, they have only carried out a few of their ideas. Lena is making a big, black bag which she calls "The Guilty Conscience of Social Democracy." She's going to fill it with everything she finds that belongs there. The audience is invited to take part.

SPEAKER (*voice over*): We announce a fantastic contest.

Various slogans are flashed on the screen.

SHARPEN YOUR MEMORY
SHARPEN YOUR MIND
WHAT IS LENA HIDING IN THE BAG?

SPEAKER (*voice over*): First prize: your own cabana in Spain. Second prize: a luxury cruise around the world. Third prize: a week of gymnastics with Princess Birgitta.

11. Lena protests

On the street, Lena, holding a microphone, scolds an opponent.

LENA: Do you really think people lose their desire to work just because of a tax increase? That they will stop working just because they don't make a hell of a lot of money? Don't you think that their *jobs* mean anything

to them? Are you that fucking stupid? Do you know what I think? (*Sounding as if the opponent had a dread disease.*) I think you're *conservative.*

From various points in Hötorget Square in the center of Stockholm, Lena, Ulla, and Magnus hold a summer clearance sale of the conservative newspaper. One after the other they call out their slogans.

LENA, ULLA, AND MAGNUS: *Svenska Dagbladet* gives you Sweden's most ancient points of view.

A newspaper with gout, *Svenska Dagbladet!*

Buy *Svenska Dagbladet,* the newspaper with gout!

An airplane passes overhead; a banner attached to it carries the slogan:

CONSERVATIVE STUDENTS

27-28 augusti

Svenska Dagbladet gives you Sweden's most ancient points of view daily.

New, improved—with gout!

Lena attacks the Great Injustice.

LENA: Some people were born with very little talent. They are lost, sort of butterfingered and brainless. Others, on the other hand, have altogether different qualifications. From the very moment they were born they had brains and talent. Should they be *rewarded* for that? So that they later on get the better jobs and the higher incomes? They get to do what they like and they have better opportunities in society. Shouldn't you *do something* about this?

Magnus pretends that he is from Expressen, *a news-*

paper that exploits political and social scandals. He stands in a doorway, talking to a middle-aged housewife.

MAGNUS: Good afternoon! I wonder if you have any interesting welfare cases in this block? People living in crummy little pads or people who have unpaid dentist bills? Junkies are okay too. You see, I'm working for *Expressen* and we are now arranging for the Conservatives to win the 1968 election. We are preparing a series

about the ten filthiest welfare cases. Could you help me out? (*The door slams.*)

Lena encounters a pessimistic doctor.

DOCTOR: Well, the class system. I guess that will always be with us.
LENA: But shouldn't we do anything about it?
DOCTOR: No, I hardly think so.
LENA: Why not?
DOCTOR (*shrugging*): Well, it turns up everywhere anyway, even where we try to get rid of it. Take Russia, for example! Now they have it again. You can have a house, you can have a profession, and many people are much better off than others, and so on.
LENA: But why shouldn't we do anything about it?
DOCTOR: Well, you can see that even under the worst conditions we have not been able to eliminate it.

Lena, Magnus, and Ulla demonstrate on the sidewalk, carrying posters.

LENA (*voice over*): I didn't like what he said, so I went to the Russian Embassy with a simple question.

One poster reads:

HAVE YOU ESTABLISHED A NEW CLASS SYSTEM?

12. Lena hates Franco

The three of them picket various travel agencies, including one which specializes in promoting tours to Spain. Their posters read:

DO YOU REMEMBER THE CIVIL WAR?
IT WAS FRANCO WHO WON
DO YOU LIKE FRANCO?
SALAZAR IS HIS BUDDY

Lena goes to Arlanda, Stockholm's airport, to try to make tourists face their responsibilities. Two planes have just landed with tourists returning from Spain. Lena confronts them.

LENA: Aren't you ashamed of going to a fascist dictatorial state?

MAN (*beaming*): Am I ashamed of going there?

LENA: Yes, aren't you ashamed?

MAN: No, absolutely not.

MAN IN FUR HAT: No, why should I be ashamed?

LENA: Because Franco is there! Because of his regime!

LADY: I think there are certain trends toward dictatorship in this country as well, when a bottle of whisky costs fifty kroner. That's a kind of dictatorship, too, you know.

LADY IN CROCHETED HAT: Yes, we were so confused. We thought of Israel for a while, but that was even more expensive . . .

LADY'S MALE COMPANION: I find it really very hard to take a stand . . .

LADY IN CROCHETED HAT: . . . so that decided it.

LENA: How do you think they're doing, the people in Spain?

ELDERLY GENTLEMAN: Oh, they're doing just fine.

LENA: Mmm.

MAN IN HAT AND GLASSES: They don't look so unhappy.

ANOTHER MAN: On Grand Canary they don't seem to be starving.

YOUNG BLONDE: They're very poor.

LENA: How do you like Franco?

MAN IN HAT AND GLASSES: I won't say anything about that.

LENA: Why not?

YOUNG MAN (*smiling*): Why should I?

LENA: Well, why shouldn't you? If you really have any opinion. Maybe you don't have one?

YOUNG MAN: No, I don't think I do.

MAN IN SUNGLASSES: I'd rather not talk about him.

LENA: Why not?

MAN IN SUNGLASSES: What?

LENA: Why not?

ANOTHER TOURIST: If you ask a Spaniard what he thinks about Franco, he'll say: "Franco is fine!"

LENA }
THE TOURIST } (*together*): Do you know what'd happen to him if he said anything else?
Quiet! Quiet, I say!

LENA: Have you ever thought about Franco?

MAN WITH SUNTAN (*seriously*): I have never even thought about you.

LENA: About Franco?

MAN WITH SUNTAN: About Franco?

LENA: What do you think of Franco?

MAN WITH SUNTAN: Do *you* know Franco?

LENA: No.

MAN WITH SUNTAN: Neither do I.

LENA: But what do you think of his politics? What do you think of his regime?

MAN WITH SUNTAN: I've been on a vacation. I haven't been talking politics.

ANOTHER BLONDE: After all, you go there to swim and rest, not to get tangled up in politics.

BALDING MAN: No, I went there for a vacation—to sunbathe and swim.

MAN IN HAT AND GLASSES: I don't care at all about such things.

LENA: No.

MAN IN FUR HAT: You forget all about it when you're down there.

LENA: Oh, you do?

MAN IN FUR HAT: You sure do.

LENA: So you just don't give a shit about it, eh?

MAN IN FUR HAT: That's right.

MAN IN DARK SHIRT: Well, I wouldn't say "shit." You just say "We're off!"

LENA: So you have no opinion?

FIRST MAN: None whatsoever.

LENA: You don't care if a whole country and all its inhabitants suffer like hell under a dictator?

FIRST MAN: No, I wouldn't say that, but I just don't want to get *involved*, that's all.

Lena, Magnus, and Ulla picket the Spanish Tourist Office.

BOYCOTT TRIPS TO SPAIN

A MALLORCA VACATION IS A SCANDAL

YOU ARE PARASITES ON THE SPANISH WORKERS

SPREAD SOCIALISM IN SPAIN!

13. The picture-frame shop

Lena needs money. After leaving Arlanda, she visits her father, Rune, at his job in an old picture-frame shop. Tired and withdrawn, Rune stands in the back room making frames.

LENA: Did you hear what I said?

RUNE: Yes. What do you want with that much money all of a sudden?

LENA: I'm going to a hypnotist!

Rune snorts.

Don't you think you ought to pay me back what you borrowed?

RUNE: Sure, but . . . Listen, don't I give you a few kroner now and then?

LENA: Yes, a few kroner now and then!

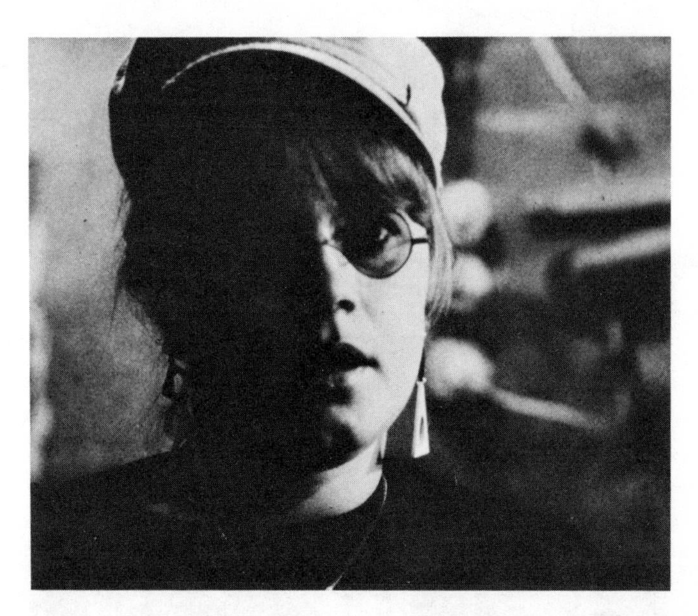

RUNE: What do you expect me to pay the rent with?
LENA (*shouting*): But I've got to have it today.

Rune tries to quiet her. She says, calmer:

You've promised me at least ten times that I'd get it back and I haven't gotten it yet.
RUNE: Sssh.
LENA: It's three months now since you borrowed it. You've said that every damn time!
RUNE: Yes, yes, all right!
LENA: Well, give it to me then!

Rune leaves the workroom and goes to the proprietor's desk at the rear of the shop.

PROPRIETOR: Listen, there's an errand to be run.
RUNE: I need a hundred in advance.
PROPRIETOR: Well, not right now.

RUNE: What's the errand?
PROPRIETOR: To the picture restorer.
RUNE: Yes, yes. (*To Lena:*) Listen! I've got to run an errand.

Contemptuously, Lena watches her father leave the shop. As she walks out, she pays no attention to a customer who has been watching her all this time: a young man who has been waiting for a newly framed watercolor.

14. Factory sabotage

Bo Holmström, a well-known television reporter, is making an imaginary Utopian TV series on the non-violent defense system which may be introduced in Sweden. Right now he's interviewing a worker in a factory outside Stockholm.

BO HOLMSTRÖM: This is foreman Evert Svensson, who is

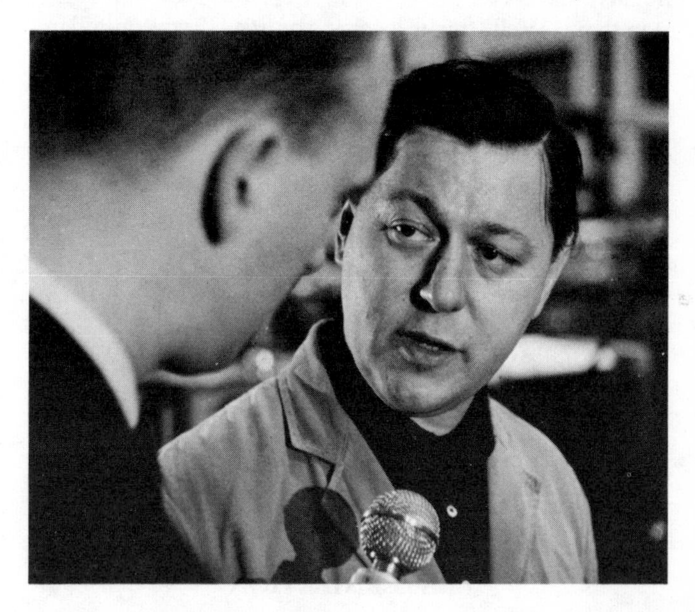

also a part of the factory defense. (*To Svensson:*) What is your job here?

SVENSSON: My job is to sabotage this machinery.

A *title appears on screen.*

SABOTAGE

HOLMSTRÖM: What kind of machinery is this?

SVENSSON: These are machines that produce these things for diesel and jet motors.
HOLMSTRÖM: Delicate things?
SVENSSON: Yes, very. There are electronic systems here that are extremely delicate.
HOLMSTRÖM: Can you explain how you'll sabotage this machinery?
SVENSSON: I can show you here.
HOLMSTRÖM: Yes.
SVENSSON: Well, this is a relay, you see. If you only damage a very small part in this relay, the whole machine will be put out of use.

NON-COOPERATION

HOLMSTRÖM: Is it hard to find the damage?
SVENSSON: Yes, very. Then it's my job to delay the repairs as long as possible.
HOLMSTRÖM: Is this just a small part of a big sabotage plan?
SVENSSON: Yes. This is just a part of it. There are many possible ways of doing it.
HOLMSTRÖM: Don't you think the enemy would get rid of you immediately if they were to occupy Sweden?
SVENSSON: Don't be too sure of that. You have to separate the idea from the individual. We shall fight the enemy's ideas . . .

FRATERNIZATION

. . . but we'll make friends with the enemy soldiers.
HOLMSTRÖM: Do you believe in non-violent defense?
SVENSSON: Yes, I do. I've taken a course in non-violent resistance, and it seems right and sensible, I think.
HOLMSTRÖM: You are a former member of the regular military defense system?

SVENSSON: Yes.
HOLMSTRÖM: But you prefer non-violence?
SVENSSON: Yes, I do. I think that if you can show how efficiently we have built up our sabotage system, the enemy will respect Sweden.
HOLMSTRÖM: Does this sabotage have serious consequences?
SVENSSON: It has enormous consequences. It prevents the new planes from flying and the new buses from running.

15. Lena meets Börje

Lena has recorded the TV program on her tape recorder, and has been listening to it as she cut out white letters to paste on the black bag. These will read:

THE GUILTY CONSCIENCE OF SOCIAL DEMOCRACY

She hears the door open.

Her father comes home. He has brought the young man from the frame shop home with him. The boy's name is Börje. But Lena doesn't want to speak to anybody. She slams her door and tells her father to go to hell. She tacks

a clipping to a shelf above her bed. It reads:

I AM FREE

Her father sets out beer and sandwiches on the kitchen table. He starts talking about Sweden's inadequate social welfare, having just read in a newspaper that several hundred blind people were discovered who had never received assistance from any organization.

RUNE: Listen! They're blind themselves.
BÖRJE: The bureaucrats?
RUNE: Sure. They're the ones who investigated this. And I wonder too why people who really can see something don't take care of them. And just think of how many there must be left of those who . . . There are lots of blind people in Sweden.
BÖRJE: Yes, yes.

RUNE: We keep sending money to all the underdeveloped countries, but why not look after your own home first, eh? What do you say about that? Why don't we look after our own country before we start talking about other countries?

BÖRJE: Oh yes, the underdeveloped countries.

RUNE: And then those people have to be retrained and given new jobs: office jobs, metalworking jobs, and darkroom jobs. Not that I know what they're trying to do but . . . Well, darkroom jobs I can understand. But a metalworker. I mean, if he stands at a lathe he has to be sensitive, so that he doesn't . . . Well, I don't know how it works.

During this conversation Lena has sauntered into the kitchen and washed down a diet pill with a glass of water. Börje eyes her with interest but she pays no atten-

tion. Finally she sits on the edge of the sink and crunches away at a piece of hard bread. Suddenly she interrupts her father and asks Börje:

LENA: What do you do?
RUNE: He works in a men's shop.

BÖRJE: At Ryden's.
LENA: Is it fun?
BÖRJE: Sometimes. It's on Kungsgatan.*
LENA: Then what's the matter?
BÖRJE: Well, your Dad and I were talking at the café about my job.
LENA: About your men's shop?
BÖRJE: Yes.
RUNE: This is a fine guy, you know.
LENA: Yeah, he may very well be, even though he works in a shop.
BÖRJE: Hey, listen! Can I have a look at your room?
RUNE: Sure, go on! But it's a mess in there.
BÖRJE: Okay?
LENA: Okay.

When Börje disappears into Lena's archive, her father takes a small roll of bills out of his pocket.

RUNE: Here's the money you were yakking about.
LENA: Where did you get it?

Rune won't answer.
Lena counts the bills. There should be 100 kroner. She throws them back at him.

Only ninety-five.
RUNE (*looks at her*): Sometimes you're too much like your mother.

During this, Börje wanders about in Lena's archive. Piles of books, walls covered with posters, boxes full of newspaper clippings and other junk. He stares amazed at a portrait of Generalissimo Franco hanging in a gilded frame surrounded by a wilted laurel wreath. That is Börje's first question when Lena comes into the room.

---

* A fashionable street.—*Trans.*

BÖRJE: Why do you have Franco on the wall?

As Lena's black bag comes into view, so does this title:

THE CONTEST

BÖRJE: What are all these boxes?
LENA: My files.
BÖRJE: And that one there? What does "R" stand for?
LENA: Religion.
BÖRJE: Well, there isn't much in it.
LENA: No, I've just started on it.
BÖRJE: "M" then?
LENA: Men!
BÖRJE: Do you collect men?
LENA: No, but I used to.

They exchange smiling glances.
In the kitchen, her father chews on a cheese sandwich.

Det hände i Stockholm:

When he goes to join the kids in the other room, he pauses in the doorway: he sees them embracing in a corner and hears them murmuring together.

BÖRJE: Hey, you're beautiful.

Rune decides to leave them in peace. But before going back to work, he picks up the money Lena refused. The door slams.

Did he leave?
LENA: Mmm. He went back to work.
BÖRJE: Maybe I should go too?
LENA (*smiles agreeably, clinging to him*): Mmm.
BÖRJE: What do you think?
LENA: Mmm.
BÖRJE: No?
LENA: Yes.

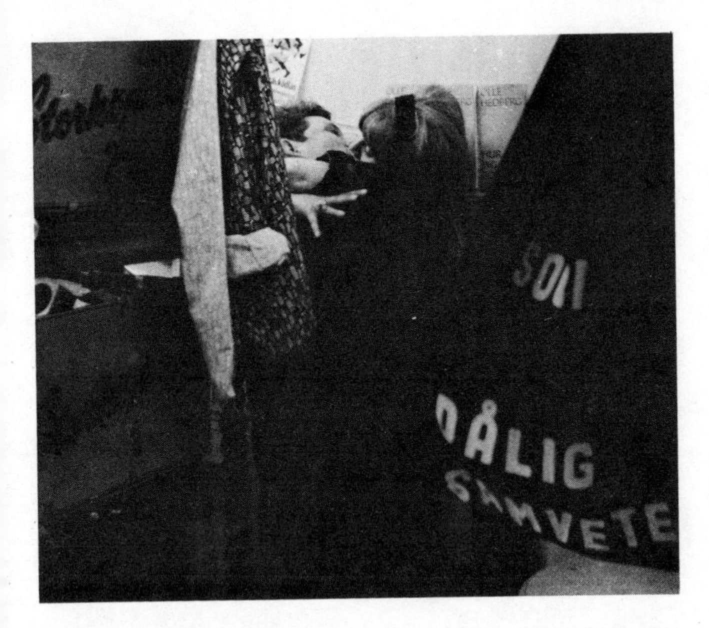

Their embraces continue. Börje can't unbutton Lena's slacks. Lena thinks that Börje is clumsy. She has to do it herself.

BÖRJE: Thank you.

Finally, they both get their pants off. Börje tries to lift Lena against the wall. Lena finds the position uncomfortable.

LENA: No.
BÖRJE: Yes.
LENA: No, it doesn't work.
BÖRJE: It doesn't?
LENA: No, it won't work.
BÖRJE: It'll work.

Lena pulls away from Börje and disappears into the closet, her panties and slacks around her ankles. There is

a terrible racket inside as cartons and boxes fall. Lena comes out with a mattress. She intends to make a bed on the floor. Börje stares in astonishment at what she is doing. His trousers are tangled around his ankles.

LENA: Help me then!

He moves the tape recorder.

God, you're slow!
BÖRJE: I'm doing my best.
LENA: Hurry up!

Magnus arrives on the stairway outside with two enormous stacks of books tied in bundles. He finds a notice on the door:

NYMAN'S INSTITUTE
CLOSED FOR LUNCH (ALL AFTERNOON)

He sits on a stool and waits for Lena to re-open her institute.

Inside, the bed is being made.

LENA: Should we have sheets?
BÖRJE: Yes, one.
LENA: Pillow?
BÖRJE: Yes, a pillow.

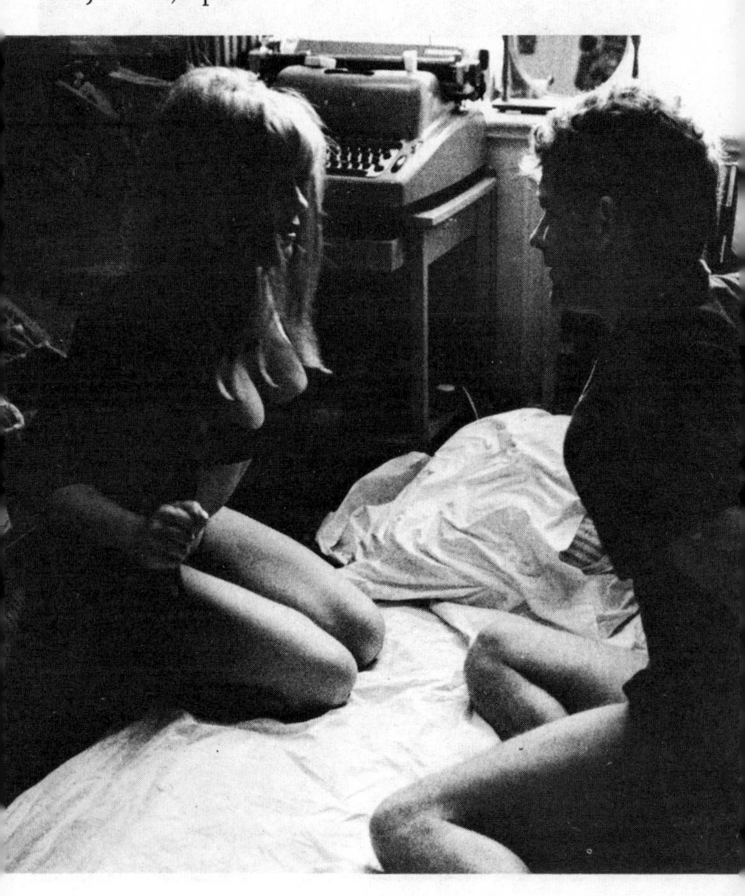

Rapid undressing. Lena's bra is twisted. Börje is only too willing to help.

No, I'll do it, I'll do it. (*When he sees Lena's breasts, he exclaims softly.*)

Lena is particular. She always takes off the boy's wrist watch before she goes to bed with him. Only then is she ready to continue their lovemaking.

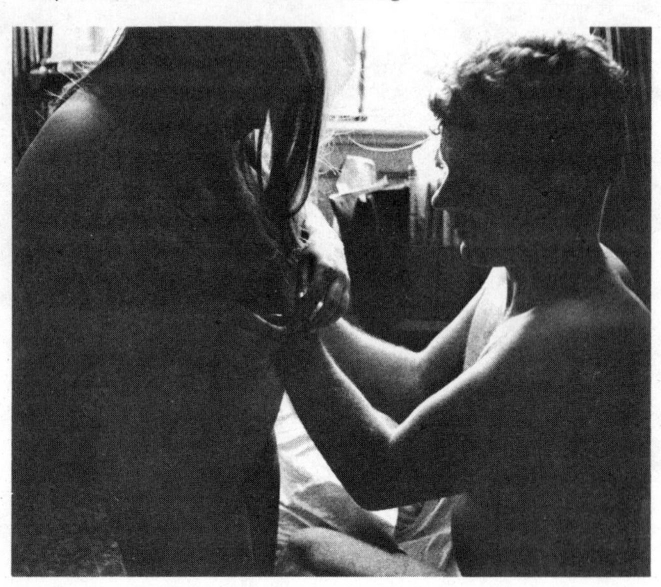

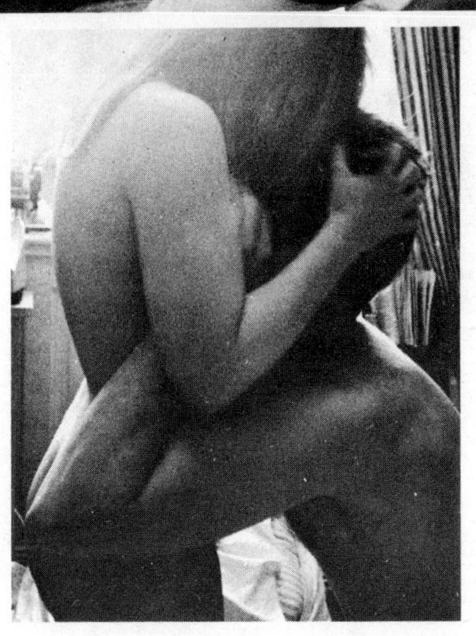

kriget

Interruption. A female announcer appears on the television screen. It seems there is a faulty coupling . . .

ANNOUNCER: We are sorry that we have had some technical difficulties in the south of Sweden during the last hour.

Late in the evening in Lena's archive. They lie on the floor, tired and naked, quieting their hunger by nibbling

on a chicken leg. Lena takes down a photograph of her father when he was young and shows it to Börje.

LENA: And a socialist. He was damned active too.
BÖRJE: Mmm.
LENA: He belonged to a lot of youth groups. And he sang.
BÖRJE: Oh, did he!
LENA: And he sang very well. And he read poems. Then he took off for Spain to fight in the Civil War. The International Brigade.

BÖRJE: I see. How long was he there?
LENA: Three weeks.
BÖRJE: Was he wounded?
LENA: No.
BÖRJE: Well, why'd he come back so soon?
LENA: I don't know.
BÖRJE: Have you asked him?
LENA: Sure, but he doesn't answer.

They prick up their ears. A doorknob is turned. Her father has come home. He hears that Lena still has a visitor and quietly closes the kitchen door. Börje rises and closes the archive door, just as discreetly. While doing this, he notices Franco's portrait again.

BÖRJE: Isn't it pretty nasty then to have Franco on the wall?
LENA: Yes.

Under the picture, Börje notices Lena's altar. Two candles, photographs from German concentration camps, and a blackboard (The Great Scandal Board), on which Lena inscribes the number of days that have passed since her father came back from Spain.

BÖRJE: Why do you have pictures from concentration camps?

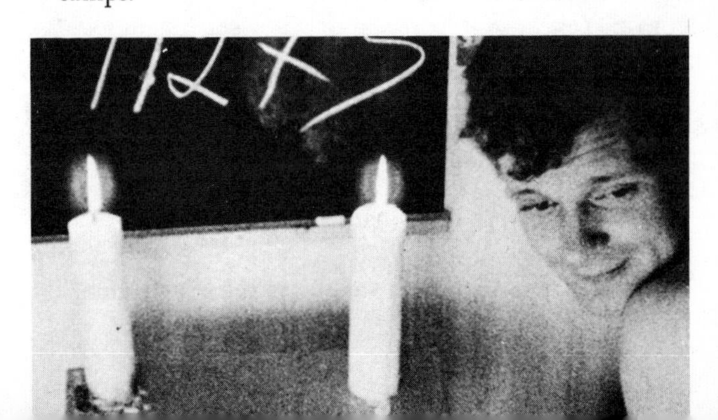

LENA: Doesn't that go together with Franco?
BÖRJE: 11,273 . . .
LENA: . . . days since he chickened out on the Spanish Civil War. *(Lena is holding a pad and pencil.)* Do you have a license?
BÖRJE: Eh?

Börje turns his head: why does she ask that? Because Lena registers the boys she sleeps with. She interviews them and enters them into a card file.

LENA: Do you have a driver's license?
BÖRJE: Yes, I have.
LENA: Did you take your first Communion?
BÖRJE: Yes, I did.
LENA: Did you ever consider refusing military service?
BÖRJE (*lies*): Yes.

Börje looks at the pictures from the Vietnam war that Lena has pinned up over her bed: soldiers, weapons, agony, torture, abandoned children.

How can you sleep with all these pictures hanging over your head?
LENA (*ignoring the question*): Do you think that women should earn the same wages as men?
BÖRJE: No.
LENA: Equal sexual freedom?
BÖRJE: Yes.
LENA: Are you married?
BÖRJE: No.
LENA: Should the Swedish Church be separated from the State?
BÖRJE: No.
LENA: Should the monarchy be abolished?
BÖRJE: No.
LENA: What party did you vote for in the last election?

BÖRJE: The Conservative.
LENA: And in the election before that?
BÖRJE: The Liberal.
LENA: Do you think that Swedish society has a class structure?
BÖRJE: No, absolutely not.
LENA: Where did you get to know my father?
BÖRJE: At the frame shop. Then we went to a café and talked. (*He takes a card at random from the file.*) Stig Björkman, born 1941, confirmed. He has a driver's license.
LENA: Did Dad borrow money from you?
BÖRJE: Yes.
LENA: I could have bet my sweet life on that.
BÖRJE (*handing her a glass of wine*): Skål, Lena! Skål!
LENA: When did you turn on to me?
BÖRJE: At the frame shop.
LENA: Do you think I was good?
BÖRJE: You were great! You were great!
LENA: How many girls have you slept with?
BÖRJE: I don't know. I've never counted them. Have you?
LENA: Mmm.
BÖRJE: Well, how many boys are there?
LENA: Twenty-three. But the first nineteen were no fun.
BÖRJE: I see.

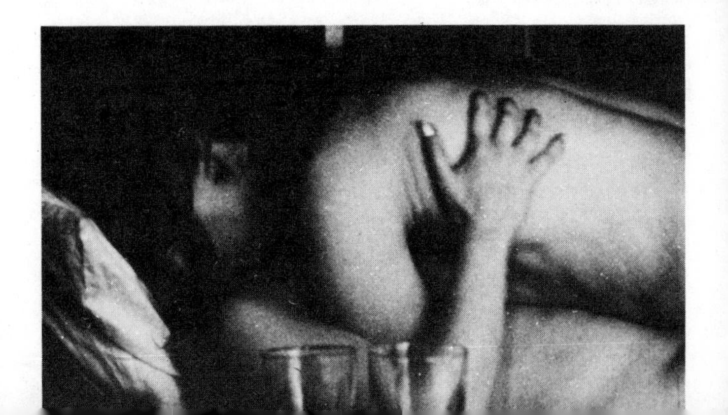

LENA: No fun.
BÖRJE: So, I'm number twenty-four?
LENA: Mmm.

?

23?

We interrupt for an imaginary special meeting at the BOARD OF FILM CENSORS *in Stockholm. When this film reaches the Board, Lena's number causes a problem. We see Mr. Erik Skoglund, 63, young film censor, checking the rules and regulations; his co-workers wonder if the number was true or to be taken as a boast. Some even begin to count on their fingers.*

DID SHE SAY 23?

In any case, Mr. Skoglund decides not to question the figure before he seeks advice from his fellow-censor, Pastor Gunnar Dahmén, a representative of the Swedish Church.

Dawn in Lena's archive. It is 1:30 A.M. *Börje coughs in his sleep, wakes up, and shivers a bit. He puts a blanket over Lena, but she awakens also.*

LENA (*whispers*): What is it?
BÖRJE (*whispers*): Hey, Lena, I'm off now.
LENA: No.
BÖRJE: I've got to go now, you see.
LENA: No, don't go.
BÖRJE: Listen, I've got to go.
LENA: No.
BÖRJE: I'm serious, I've got to leave. It's late! Listen Lena, I've got to run now. You lie down and go back to sleep.
LENA: No, I'll come with you.
BÖRJE: Okay, but make it quick, make it . . .
LENA: Mmm.
BÖRJE: You've got to make it quick. Clothes on, quickly.
LENA: Mmm. Mmm.

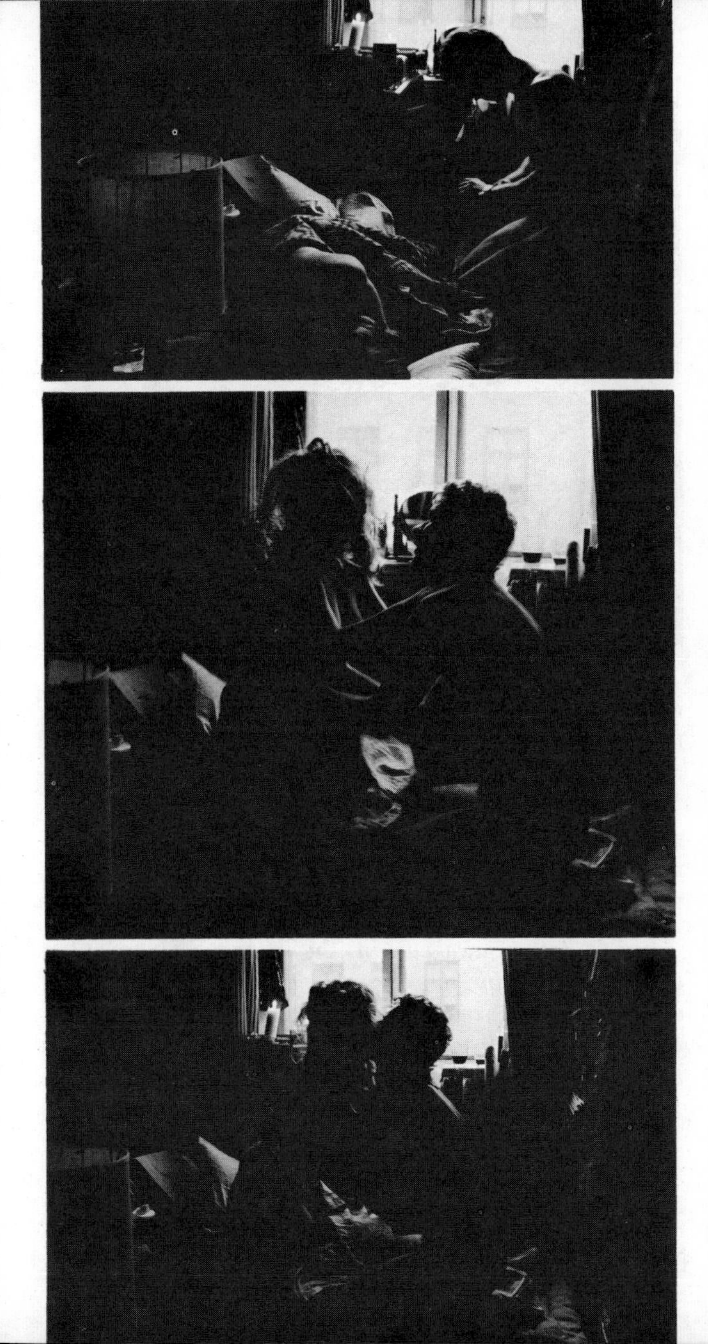

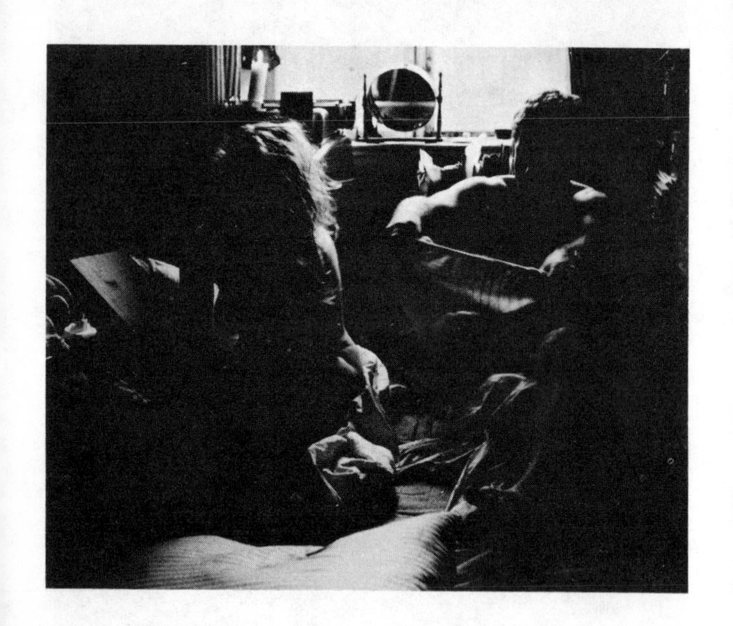

BÖRJE: Quickly.
LENA: Mmm.
BÖRJE: Where are my trousers? Where the hell are my trousers?
LENA: And my bra?
BÖRJE: You can go without one.
LENA: Yes.

Lena's father awakens in the kitchen. He wanders sleepily to the sink and pisses in the basin. Some voices are heard in the courtyard: good friends of his who want to come up for a beer. But he waves them away. He can't have them up when Lena has a boyfriend in there.

Because it is a new day Lena must change 11,273 to 11,274 before she steals out with Börje. Her father, by the sink, nods in a friendly way.

Once he hears them leave, he waves to his friends in the

yard. It's okay now! Come on up! The kids are gone!

This is Tuesday, June 14. Sunrise 2:35 A.M. Temperature in Stockholm 62° F. And with Börje in back on the luggage carrier, Lena cycles through an empty Stockholm at dawn.

They pause by the Royal Palace and watch the changing

of the guard. Leaning over the stone balcony, they regard the quietness.

LENA *(croons)*: "In Rio de Janeiro you can *folk* for free . . ."

Panoramic views of the Parliament, the biggest banking houses, the Opera, the Grand Hotel, various waterways, and a crowd of seagulls chattering as they pass.

LENA *(voice over)*: Now the Prime Minister gets up to take care of Sweden.

And the Minister of Trade wakes up.

And all the Lefties.

And the whole mixed economy.

The Conservative party leader rubs his eyes because he's had a nightmare.

And Torsten Eriksson * gets up and makes pee-pee; and begins devising another defense of the new State Prison at Kumla.

And Per Wrigstad † vomits again in *Expressen.*

Börje thinks. He thinks that he and Lena have been together exactly half a day, from lunch yesterday. Shall they end the idyll here? Put the finishing touches on the masterwork, the cork in the bottle, so to speak?

He whispers his idea in Lena's ear. She gladly nods yes. Börje takes off his jacket; Lena takes off her panties. A watching Palace guard swallows, his Adam's apple bobbing. After Börje places his jacket over Lena's shoulders, they swing up onto the balustrade in front of the Palace and rock in each other's arms, while the guard continues to watch impassively.

---

* The Head of the Bureau of Prisons who is under heavy attack from Swedish radicals for blocking further reforms.—*Trans.*

† The editor-in-chief, who uses his newspaper for vulgar anti-socialist propaganda. His favorite target: Olof Palme.—*Trans.*

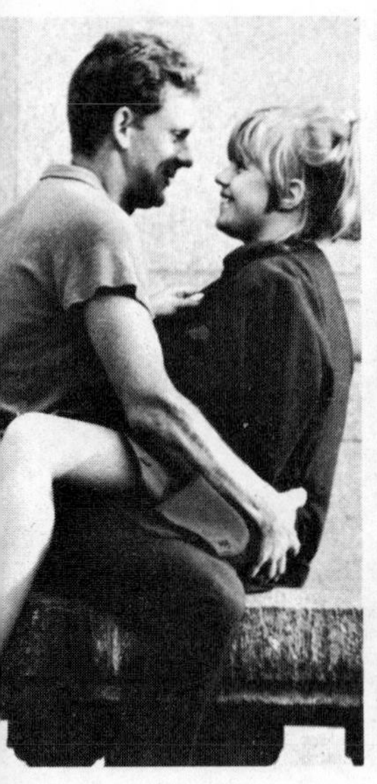

A choir sings the national anthem, "The King's Song."
"From the depth of Swedish hearts we sing
A simple hymn unto our King.
Show faith in him! Don't let him down!
Lighten the burden of his crown!"
And Lena wonders how things are going with the King. Why not go into the Palace and interview him?

16. Lena comforts the King

An imaginary interview.

There is a collection of family portraits on a table in one of the Palace chambers. One is of Carl Gustaf, the crown prince, who looks remarkably like Börje.

His Majesty is walking through the chambers of the Palace, a suitcase in each hand; a Pekinese trots after him. A music box is playing softly. He has just finished his long service, now that the Kingdom of Sweden has been turned into a republic. The court has been pensioned off. Now he needs his grandson to help with his departure.

THE KING: Carl Gustaf, where are you?

Lena hurries up, microphone in hand.

LENA: Is there anything I can do?

THE KING: No, it's all right. I'm ready. Is it chilly outside?

LENA: No, Your Majesty, it's a nice Swedish summer morning.

THE KING: A bit chilly then.

LENA: Yes, a bit.

THE KING: If only Carl Gustaf would come with the tickets. He promised to take care of them. The last thing he was to do yesterday was to go to the travel agency.

LENA: I know that I'm intruding. But may I just ask what it feels like?

THE KING: What it feels like? What do you mean?

LENA: We've had kings in Sweden for a billion years. How does it feel to be absolutely the last one?

THE KING: If you give me a moment to consider, I'll find an answer for you. (*He sets down his bags.*) Well, it's like this: It's important to separate the idea from the individual. That's something we have to learn from early childhood. I've been trying all my life to separate these two things. I've really made an effort. (*He picks up his bags.*) But sometimes it's difficult. Very difficult.

LENA: But Nancy Eriksson * explained it on TV, and all the socialists said it too: It isn't *you* as a *person* they wanted to get at. On the contrary, you have been an outstanding representative of . . .

THE KING: Yes, yes, I know.

And then it happens. In comes the "Prince." And he looks remarkably *like Börje.*

A VOICE: Grandfather!

THE KING: Yes, I'm here. Where have you been? I thought you had forgotten . . .

* The Social Democratic Party in Sweden has always had as part of its program: Abolish the Kingship. However, the issue was shelved for several decades. Not until the mid-sixties was it taken down and dusted off. A group of M.P.'s led by Nancy Eriksson moved for an investigation of the "Kingship question."—*Trans.*

BÖRJE (*as Crown Prince Carl Gustaf*): Well, I . . . Here they are anyway.

He gives the plane tickets to his "Grandfather," the King; then turns to Lena and whispers.

BÖRJE (*as the Prince*): It's been delightful meeting you, Lena, but I'm tired, so I've got to take a nap. (*Börje as Börje.*) We're having a sale at Ryden's, you see. (*As the Prince again.*) Delightful meeting you.

LENA: But what about *you?* How do you feel? Just think of not being able to be anything but a crown prince.

BÖRJE: I don't give a damn about that! (*Walks away, pauses, turns.*) Will you call me?

LENA: Where?

BÖRJE: At Ryden's. It's in the phone book. (*He disappears.*)

THE KING: I hope it's nice in Italy now. Not too hot. At the airport in Rome it's usually . . .

LENA: I think it's just great down there now. I wouldn't mind going myself, if only I could get away, but with the Institute and all the investigations . . . Come along! Mind the step, now. (*To the Pekinese.*) Is your master taking you to Italy? . . .

17. Marie

The same morning. A small apartment. A blonde young woman is brushing the hair of her three-year-old daughter before giving her breakfast. A key turns in the lock.

MARIE: Who's coming? Who's coming?
GIRL: Daddy?
MARIE: Yes.

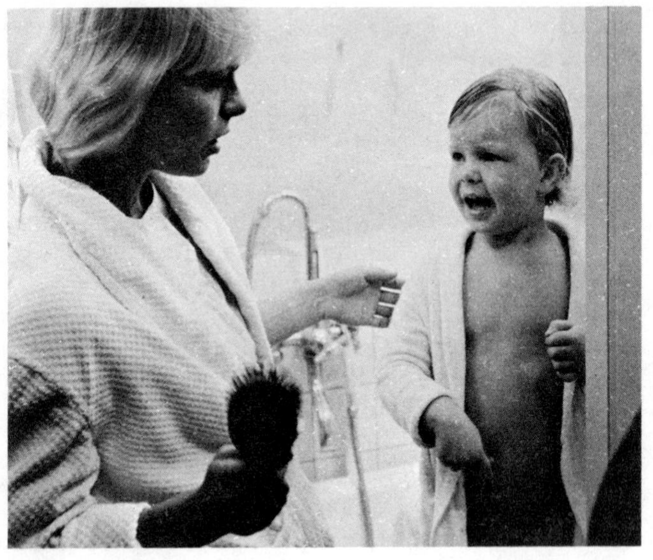

BÖRJE: Hello.
MARIE: Hello.
GIRL: Daddy?
MARIE: Yes.
GIRL: It is Daddy.
MARIE: Yes, it is Daddy.
A VOICE FROM THE RADIO: Sartre meant that the Tribunal would investigate what sentences should be passed if

SVERIGE
TROTT
USA

NI
VET
VARFÖR

NU
SKÄMS
VI

uths chanting "U.S.A. murderers! U.S.A. murderers! S.A. murderers!" Many of the signs read:

U.S.A. GET OUT OF VIETNAM!

Lena also makes new posters for the communist em- ıssies.

I LIKE COMMUNISM WITHOUT SLAVE CAMPS
I LIKE SOCIALISM WITHOUT TYRANNY

ENA (*voice over*): The next day we went to the Chinese Embassy at Bragevägen. After that I went to the Russian Embassy to talk to the Ambassador himself; he wasn't in.

But Yevtushenko was there. He said that my signs were ridiculous.

Lena gets very upset and has an imaginary interview th Yevtushenko and his interpreter.

NA: What! What does he mean?

ERPRETER: Well, what he means is very simple. Milions of people all over the world today are starving, ving under conditions so miserable that you, Lena Jyman, would never accept them—not even for five ninutes. Now, if you chose the capitalistic solution—en you have free enterprise, free speech, and a lot of her good things. But that development would take

the laws used at the Nüremburg trials were applied to the aggressors in Vietnam.

"We represent no government, no party, and therefore we take orders from no one." These were Jean-Paul Sartre's words at the opening of the Russell Tribunal in Stockholm.

"We are powerless," he said, "and in that lies the guarantee of our independence."

Börje turns off the radio. He stretches out on the bed, tired after being awake all night with Lena. In the kitchen, Marie empties the contents of a can into a bowl in front of the child.

GIRL: No, I want food.
MARIE: But this is food. Now eat like a good girl! (*To Börje:*) Would you like something too? A sandwich?
BÖRJE: Yes, please.
MARIE: A beer?
BÖRJE: Mmm.

Marie takes a beer from the refrigerator. Börje gives her a package. It is the picture he had picked up at the frame shop the day before during his lunch hour. Marie recognizes the watercolor. She painted it a few years ago. She is shy but a little moved by his thoughtfulness.

MARIE: Did you frame this?
BÖRJE: Like it?
MARIE: I paint a lot better now.
BÖRJE: Yes, but it's nice.
MARIE: Yes, we had a wonderful time that afternoon, anyway.
BÖRJE: Are you happy?
MARIE: Yes.

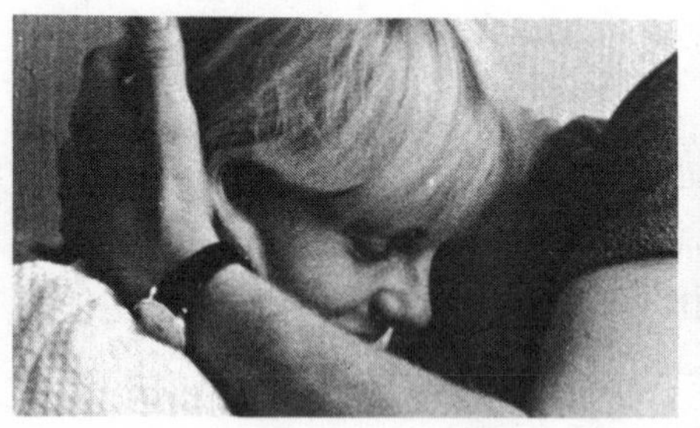

Börje kisses Marie. Their daughter laughs, delighted.

18. Lena and The Universal Pro

LENA (*voice over*): Occasionally, I was neglig The Great Scandal Board. But all of a sudd thing would remind me of how my old man c out on the Spanish Civil War and . . .

The count on the board increases: 11,274, 11,276, etc., through 11,283.

Besides, I think that you should make your clear to the world. So Ulla, Magnus, and I wer big embassies. In front of the American Embas was a police car. There was always a police ca all summer.

Their signs say:

EVEN SWEDEN ONCE BELIEVED IN THE U.S.

NOW WE ARE ASHAMED

DO YOU KNOW WHY?

LENA (*voice over*): I told the police that I was looking for trouble, simply taking an intellectu tion. But since the cops didn't understand th ence, it was quite a short demonstration.

Lena joins a protest march of writers, stude

300 years.

LENA: So let it then.

Yevtushenko responds in dismay and disbelief.

INTERPRETER: But don't you see? It has to be done in thirty years. In thirty years illiteracy must be eliminated. In thirty years the country must be industrialized—and

you think this could be done without compulsion!

No! But Lena, you mustn't forget that compulsion isn't the same to you as it is to them. They've had the whip over them for a thousand years, so another thirty years doesn't mean a thing, as long as they believe there will really be a change.

LENA: But what about the purges and the murders! And people being deported? The slave camps? *(To the in-*

terpreter:) Look at his country under Stalin! He has written poetry himself about the terror they endured. Can he deny that? (*To Yevtushenko:*) Can you deny that?

INTERPRETER: No, he doesn't deny that. He says it is sad that the new Soviet had to be born with so much sacrifice, but one has to take risks.

LENA: Risks! Doesn't he realize what hideous risks he's talking about?

INTERPRETER: Oh yes, he certainly does. But realizing that millions of people are starving to death, do you think that's taking less of a hideous risk?

Lena looks down, ashamed.

LENA (*voice over*): Well, there I was with my fear of the Russians and the Chinese, and what she said was probably right. That was more than I could take.

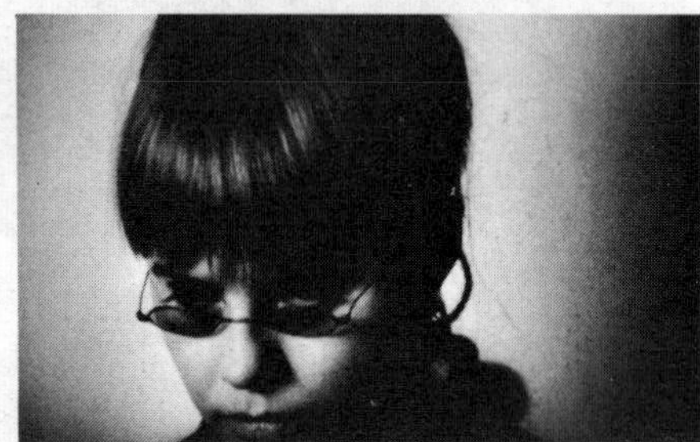

19. A cosy evening

Lena is with her father in the frame shop. He has been working late. Now he's washing up. He turns his shirt inside-out before going out to grab a bite to eat. Lena is hand-printing little cards for her files, but cuts the board incorrectly.

RUNE: When my old man died, I was with . . . No, wait a minute, wait now. You mustn't do it that way, don't you realize that it's much harder that way! You should only draw a fine line first. Like this, see? You do it like this! Then you press hard. Like this. (*Continues his story.*) Yes, when my old man died, I was in the room lying beside him in the bed. He lay there, tossing and turning, and I woke up twice during the night. I only thought he was a little restless, but when I woke up the next morning his neck had turned blue.

LENA: Do you think animals feel the same way as we do when they die?
RUNE: Oh yes, sure they do. I was at a bullfight in Spain once, and I almost puked. I had to leave. Oh, come on, have some wine! (*He hands her the bottle; then he takes a drink himself.*)
LENA: What do you think of Börje?
RUNE: Mmm.
LENA: Do you like him?
RUNE: Mmm.
LENA: He's kind of groovy.
RUNE: Yes, he's a fine boy.
LENA: Mmm. I'm getting kind of turned on to him. (*She giggles.*)
RUNE (*laughs*): Do you think I didn't see anything through the door before I left that day?

LENA (*laughing*): No!
RUNE: Oh yes, I did!
LENA: No!
RUNE: Oh yes!
LENA: I see.
RUNE: But listen, what's important with that guy is that . . . At the café before . . . well, he talked so nicely about his child. He talked so nicely about her.

Lena's father doesn't notice that she suddenly looks gloomy.

Just like I felt about you when you were little and your mother ran off.
LENA: Oh, that bitch!
RUNE: Oh well, she was all right . . .
LENA: No, she wasn't—showing up after eight years and wanting me back!

RUNE (*sings*): "Here I sat on the river bank—
I'm singing, tra la la . . . to myself—
Listening to the river surging in the valley—
I hear him calling—"

LENA: What's her name, that woman?

RUNE (*sings*): ". . . tra la la . . ."
What?

LENA: The kid's mother?

RUNE: I think it was Marie or something like that. (*Sings:*)
"I'll take my violin—
Let the river be my bass—"

LENA (*in a sudden outburst*): What the hell does he want with me then, when he's got both Marie and . . . That damn . . .

RUNE: Yes, but listen, you've been experimenting yourself!

LENA: Yes, but that's a completely different thing! At least I say when I'm experimenting! But that bastard hasn't said a thing! Everybody else . . . Hell, even *you* know! But I don't . . .

RUNE (*sings*): "Dear old river surging in the valley
We are old, you and I, and rather gray.
Girls want young lovers

Who are fast and light on their feet.
Our days are over . . ."

Lena, melancholy, gently straightens the collar of her father's inside-out shirt.

LENA: Have you put it on inside out again?
RUNE (*sings*): ". . . And in our nook we sit and watch
The young people dancing.

Our days are over.
And in our nook we sit and watch
The young people dancing."

20. A TV program

ANNOUNCER (*on screen*): We regret having to interrupt this program with a message.

BO HOLMSTRÖM (*in a studio*): After one of the most intensive debates that the Swedish government has experienced, we can now give you the results of the vote on the new radical defense system.

There was a strong majority for the system in the

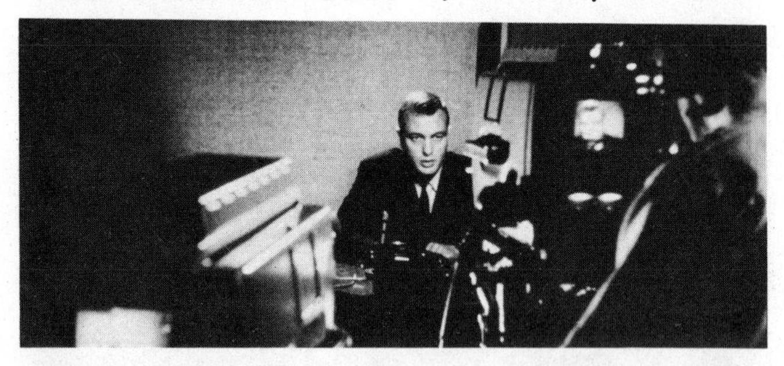

Social Democratic Party. Also, the Communists were very much in favor of the non-violent defense system, but the Conservatives were very much opposed. The final total is 187 opposed and 196 in favor, which means that the new non-violent defense system is hereby decided upon. This means a four-month course in non-violent techniques for all citizens and one month of repetition every three years; and for the first time in Swedish history this applies to both men and women.

Various shots of demonstrations and police. A shot of the plane with the CONSERVATIVE STUDENTS *banner.*

Even at the last minute there were violent debates over the reform. Some groups among the students turned out to be unexpectedly conservative.

Shots of young men and women struggling in the snow.

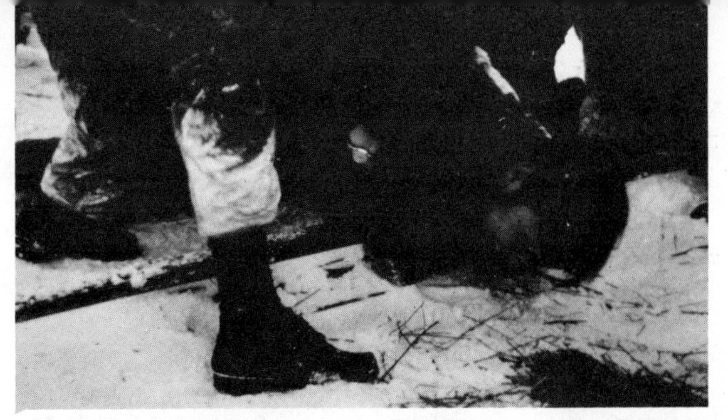

ANNOUNCER (*voice over*): Last winter we visited with some new recruits and on that day's schedule it read: "Sociodrama." This was one of the first exercises for newly drafted youngsters. Their mission was to block a railway track.

A MALE VOICE: What would you do if it were your wife lying here on the tracks, you silly fool . . .

NON-VIOLENT OFFICER: Break it up! Time for self-criticism!

Get up! I shut up! You speak!

FIRST NON-VIOLENT SOLDIER: I think this whole exercise is unreal. I don't think this situation would take place—I mean, that they would come unarmed like this.

SECOND NON-VIOLENT SOLDIER: I agree.

FIRST NON-VIOLENT SOLDIER: This is too simplified a situation for us.

THIRD NON-VIOLENT SOLDIER: I mean, if the situation were critical—that is, if a train loaded with ammunition were coming this way—who cares if a few people are lying on the tracks?

HOLMSTRÖM (*approaches the group*): Am I allowed to take part in the self-criticism? Isn't it hard to restrain yourself from striking back?

FOURTH NON-VIOLENT SOLDIER: Yes, it's incredibly hard—even during exercises like this one.

HOLMSTRÖM: Is it possible through training to eliminate your aggressive feelings when maybe it's your fiancée who is being shot?

FIRST NON-VIOLENT SOLDIER: I think so.

HOLMSTRÖM: And you don't feel like a coward?

FIRST NON-VIOLENT SOLDIER: No!

HOLMSTRÖM: So after all you are gladly taking part in this?

NON-VIOLENT GIRL: Well, gladly . . .

HOLMSTRÖM: In the days of the old defense system, women didn't have to take part, but now they must. What do you think about that?

NON-VIOLENT GIRL: I'm all for it. Why should only men defend themselves? I think it's . . . I don't see why *he* should just sit there and get shot.

HOLMSTRÖM (*to the instructor*): To a spectator this looks like a scout camp, rather than a realistic war or occupation.

NON-VIOLENT OFFICER: No, I think this is just as realistic

as ordinary military exercises. Those too can remind you of scout camps or playing cowboys and Indians. I can't see any difference.

HOLMSTRÖM: Part of the idea is to make friends with the enemy soldiers as people, right?

NON-VIOLENT OFFICER: Yes, just like during World War I, when the soldiers left their respective trenches and exchanged cigarettes and made friends with each other.

A title appears on the screen.

FRATERNIZATION

HOLMSTRÖM: This means that you'll make friends . . .

SABOTAGE

. . . with the enemy. But, don't you thereby . . .

. . . open your front to their propaganda?

NON-VIOLENT OFFICER: Yes, of course, but we also make it possible for them to receive ours. And that's what's most important. We must always be open.

HOLMSTRÖM: Would you say that it's those with the strongest characters who can take the greatest strain?

NON-VIOLENT OFFICER: Roughly, I'd say that those who can stand the greatest strain in a conventional war can also stand the strain in this. (*A train whistle sounds.*) Now, my friends, we will change sides! Those who were the defenders down here will now be the aggressors, and vice versa. It's important that those who are the aggressors really feel the pleasure, the excitement of violence, so that you get to experience it in reality. Okay, let's begin!

CHORUS (*voice over*): "We shall . . ."

NON-VIOLENT OFFICER: Change groups! Go ahead!

CHORUS: ". . . overcome some day."

NON-VIOLENT OFFICER: Hurry up . . .

CHORUS: "We shall . . ."

NON-VIOLENT OFFICER: . . . so we don't get too stiff.

CHORUS: ". . . overcome."

NON-VIOLENT OFFICER: We're all frozen stiff . . .

CHORUS: "We shall . . ."

NON-VIOLENT OFFICER: . . . already.

CHORUS: ". . . overcome."

NON-VIOLENT OFFICER: Ready!

CHORUS: "We shall . . ."

NON-VIOLENT OFFICER: Go!

CHORUS: ". . . overcome.
We shall overcome some day."

21. Lena takes a bicycle ride

The count on The Great Scandal Board increases from 11,289 to 11,304.

Lena has left Stockholm. She rides her bicycle down a country road thinking about the possibilities of the non-violent defense system and humming with great confidence.

LENA: ". . . deep in my heart
I do believe
we shall overcome some day."

Suddenly a car from Stockholm roars by. The road is full of puddles and the driver ruthlessly splashes water all over the girl.

Lena is furious and yells after him:

LENA: Oh, you Stockholm bastard! Go to hell! Road maniac! Damned road maniac! Go to h . . . Oh shit! You big shit! (*Her cursing goes on and on.*)

22. Lena tells the people

In every little village or town she passes through during her ride through Sweden, Lena posts messages on trees and walls. For example:

MESSAGE TO HUMANITY:
DOWN WITH PRIVILEGED SOCIETIES!

—LENA

MESSAGE TO BLACK PEOPLE:
BE PREPARED! THE WHITES ARE STAGGERING!

—LENA

23. The rivals

Börje suddenly decides to visit Lena. When he arrives she is not there. Instead, he runs into a stranger in Lena's archive. The stranger is Magnus and they are both equally surprised.

MAGNUS: Hello! Who are you?
BÖRJE: Check the files! Number 24.
MAGNUS: What are you doing here?
BÖRJE: Lena was looking for me at my job one day when I wasn't there. Now I'd like to know where she is. Do you know where she is?
MAGNUS: Yes.
BÖRJE: Where?
MAGNUS: She's on a retreat.
BÖRJE: What?
MAGNUS: A retreat! Do you know what that is? A *retreat*!

Börje gets aggressive. He knocks Magnus down and grabs him by the hair.

flicka
som styr
Kennedy!

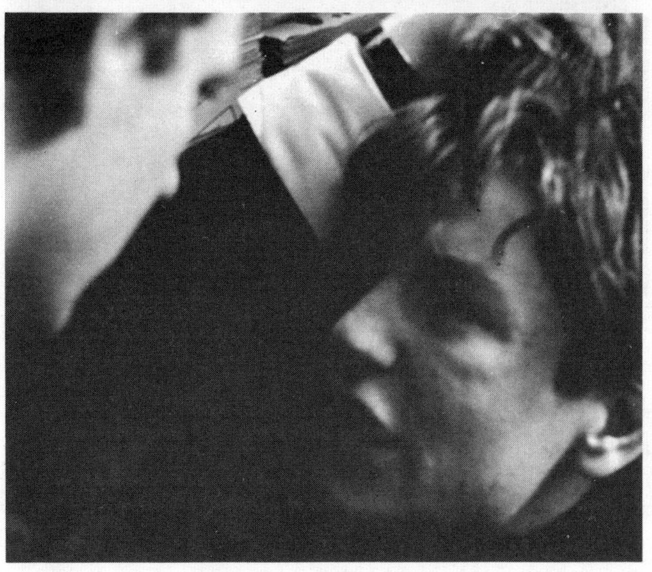

BÖRJE: I asked where Lena was.
MAGNUS: She wants to be left alone.
BÖRJE: Yes, yes! She wanted to see me. What are you doing here?
MAGNUS: What am I doing! I live here.
BÖRJE: What?
MAGNUS: I live here. I've been told to stay here and take care of the place.
BÖRJE: Has Lena left town?
MAGNUS: I don't know! I told you she wants to be left alone. What in hell do you come barging in here for? I've told you that Lena wants to be left alone, that I live here, and that I don't know where she is.
BÖRJE: You're lying!
MAGNUS: No!
BÖRJE (*slapping him*): You're lying!
MAGNUS: No!

Lena's father has appeared in the doorway.

RUNE: Hey, what are you doing?
BÖRJE: Listen, where is Lena?
RUNE: In Småland.
BÖRJE: Where in Småland?
RUNE: At Rumskulla.
BÖRJE: Thank you.

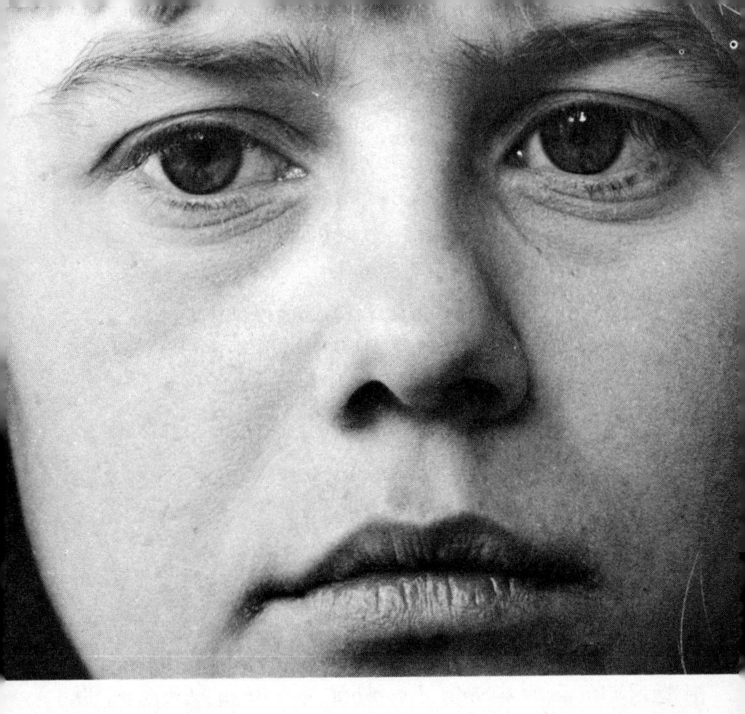

24. Lena on a retreat

Lena has withdrawn to an isolated place in southern Sweden. She has rented an old abandoned cottage. She has an ambitious program during her retreat:

6:15 MEDITATION

In order to come closer to nature, she gets up early and meditates on a bluebell.

7:30 BREAKFAST

As an Indian steps into the healing waters of the Ganges, she wades into the Stångå and fills a bowl with fresh water for her morning meal.

9:00–12:00 MEDITATION ON LARS GYLLENSTEN'S TEN COMMANDMENTS

In response to the question "Are God's Ten Commandments Enough?" the Swedish author, Lars Gyllensten, has written a set of ten commandments for this age. The walls of Lena's house are covered with posters copied from this book. She reads:*

THIRD COMMANDMENT:
THOU SHALT REFLECT THAT COMFORT AGREES AS WELL WITH OTHER PEOPLE AS IT DOES WITH YOU.
FIRST COMMANDMENT:
THOU SHALT NOT HAVE ANY OTHER GODS THAN PROVISORY ONES.

12:45 LUNCH

For lunch Lena has three peas, which she eats carefully.

1:00 STUDIES

In honor of Martin Luther King, she has built an altar to NON-VIOLENCE*—central symbol: a broken shotgun. She reads his writings and studies the techniques of non-violence.*

2:10 FIGHT AGAINST NONSENSE

Consists of various activities; for example, burning magazines.

3:00–5:00 SELF-MORTIFICATION

She is making a bed of nails. She meditates over a piece of banana cream cake in order to learn to stay away from sweets.

6:30 DINNER

She savors and then noisily gobbles a whole carrot.

* These have been published in English in *Sweden Writes* (Stockholm: Bokförlaget, 1965).—*Trans.*

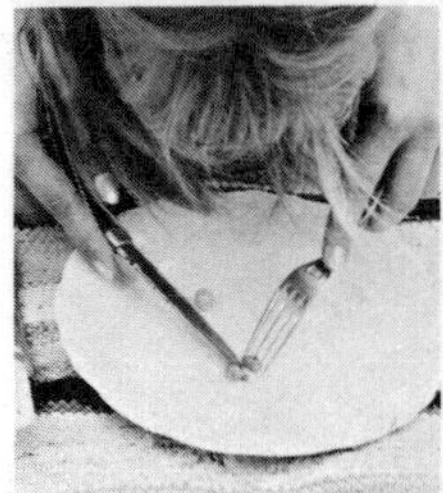

ICKE-VÅLD
MARTIN LUTHER KING OCH LENA

10:05 SEXUAL THEORY

Upon retiring, she studies recently published sex manuals. One illustrates fresh, unusual positions, guaranteed to brighten a conventional everyday relationship. She finds this sort of meditation difficult all by herself.

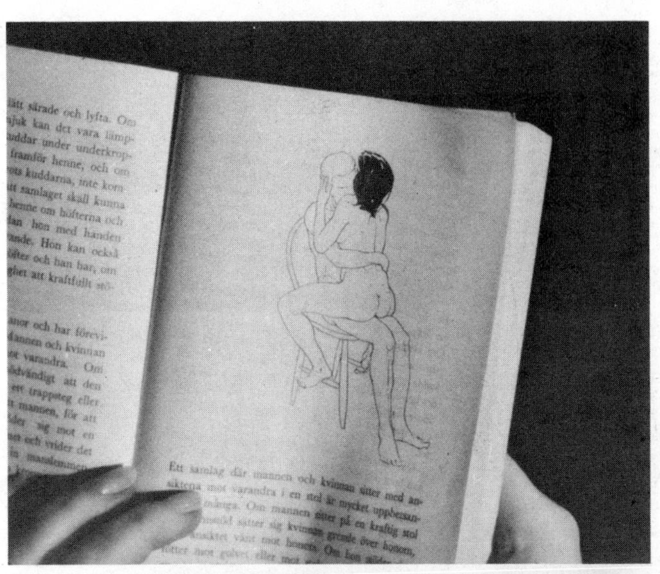
Ett samlag där mannen och kvinnan sitter med an-

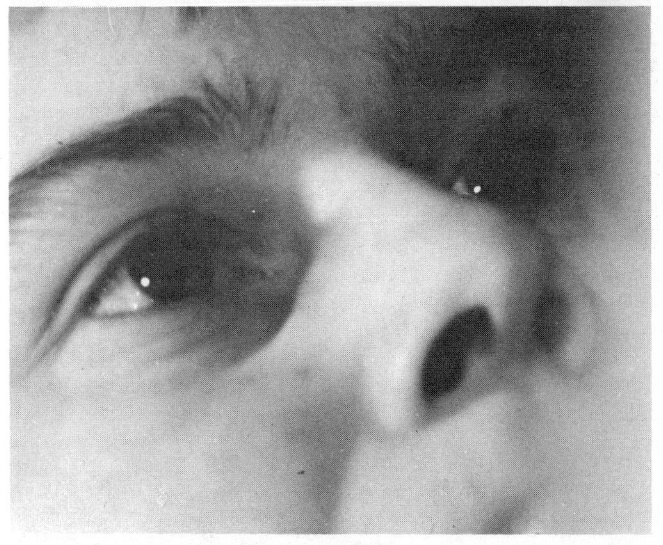

intill sig. Denna ställning kan också få den utform-
ningen att kvinnan ligger intill sängkanten och mannen står på golvet intill sängen.
Den följande klassiska ställningen, känd både från

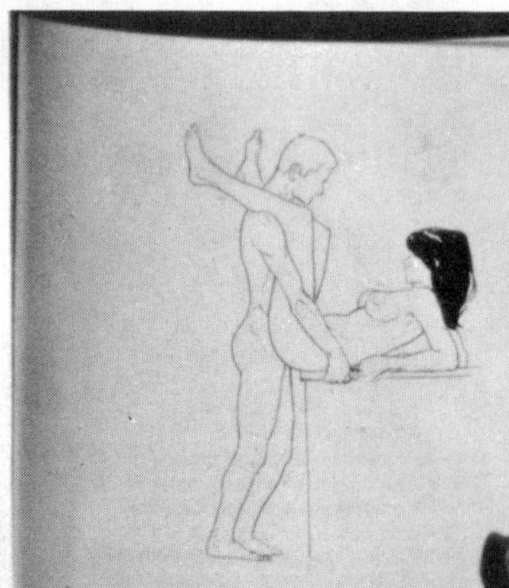
komma till stånd med hjälp av varje möbel som ä
hög nog för att föra könsdelarna i det nära läge som
erfordras.
Tidigare har en sittande ställning beskrivits, där
mannen och kvinnan sitter ansikte mot ansikte me
benen kring varandra. Den följande variationen
kräver en rätt hård bädd – men den går bra att ut-

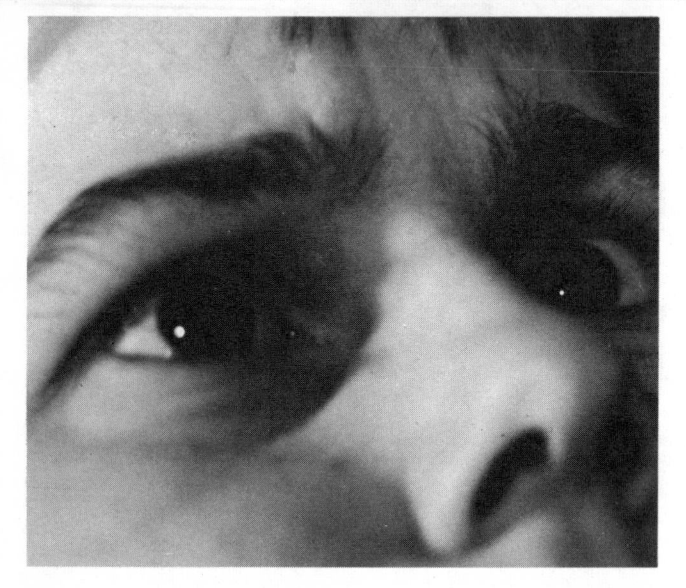

9:00 A.M. DIALECT STUDY

She usually goes to get milk from two middle-aged brothers whose dialect is so peculiar that she can translate their speech only by diligent effort.

LENA: Do you ever go to church?

FIRST BROTHER (*in incomprehensible dialect*): No, I don't.

LENA: Why?

FIRST BROTHER (*in incomprehensible dialect*): Because they don't preach the truth, for example. They pray so beautifully for the poor, but you know very well what they're really like.

LENA: Would you like to have a woman around the house to help you?

SECOND BROTHER (*in incomprehensible dialect, grinning*): Oh, yes, of course I would, but another of my brothers used to be here and cook for us. There were always

complaints about everything. We never had time to get home and eat when he was cooking. We were always several kilometers from here when the meals were ready.

10:00–12:00 YOGA EXERCISE

On a mat in front of the house, she attempts to follow the instructions in a yoga book. But the positions are too difficult. So, in the midst of her solitude, she turns to the film crew.

LENA: No, I can't make it.

The film crew begins showing Lena positions she might try.

LENA MALMSJÖ: You needn't do that particular position. There are lots of others. This one, for example.

Lena Malmsjö, executive producer, executes a backbend. Vilgot Sjöman performs a yogi shoulder stand.

VILGOT: Nyman! Have a look! But loo . . . And then just straight up, you stretch them like this. Is that okay?

Everybody helps. Cameraman Peter Wester and his assistant Andreas Bellis; sound engineer Tage Sjöborg and his assistant Christer Östberg; script girl Marianne Johnson; general assistant Bengt Palmers, and production manager Raymond Lundberg—they all demonstrate positions for Lena. Each is identified by a subtitle.

25. Wild West in Fagerdal

Börje roars through Småland in a new white MG. He drives into Lena's yard. She grabs the shotgun from the altar to non-violence, loads it, and stalks him, as in a cowboy film.

He grabs the gun from her and dumps her in the grass. He lays his head in her lap and drinks, as if from a well.

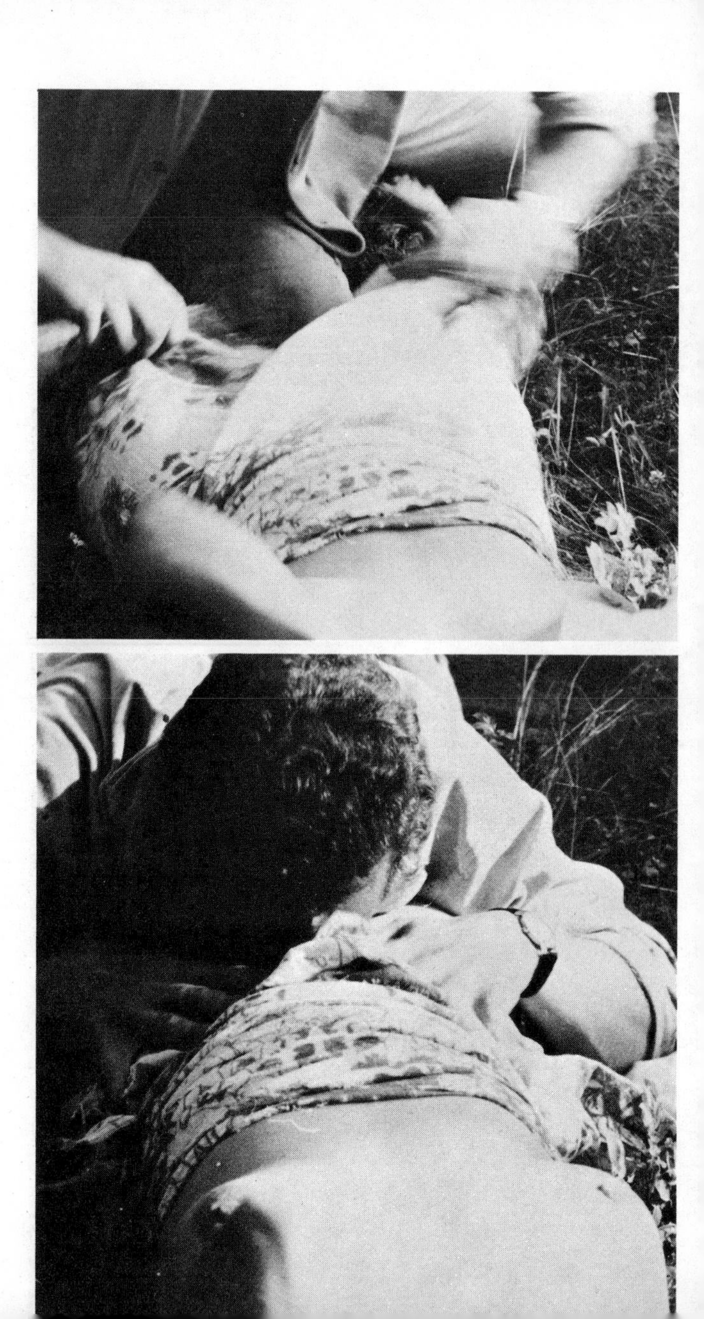

Some time later they lie, exhausted, their bodies satisfied, sprawled in the grass. Börje caresses her side, she kisses his penis: small, light, childishly contented kisses.

BÖRJE: I had trouble finding you.
LENA: Have you done much looking?
BÖRJE: Yes, I have.
LENA: What a nice car you have.

BÖRJE: You think so?
LENA: Mmm.
BÖRJE: I've got a new job.
LENA: Mmm.
BÖRJE: I quit Ryden's.
LENA: What are you doing now?
BÖRJE: I sell cars. . . . What have you been doing all this time?

26. Sightseeing at Rumskulla

Lena shows Börje all the discoveries she has made at Rumskulla during her retreat. She shows him how people used to live in the past, in solitude, deep in the forests.

LENA: Here's the doorstep. Here they went in and out, Hulda, Alma, Oscar, Selma, Emil, Emilia, Amanda, and all the children. In 1882, 1883, 1884 . . .

BÖRJE: Hey, what are these stones?

LENA: That's the stove. And this is all there was to the house.

Börje has brought a present for Lena: a small bracelet. Lena is moved and kisses him.

The director, who is watching them, gets a little disturbed and caresses the script girl.

Lena and Börje are parked on a hill with a beautiful

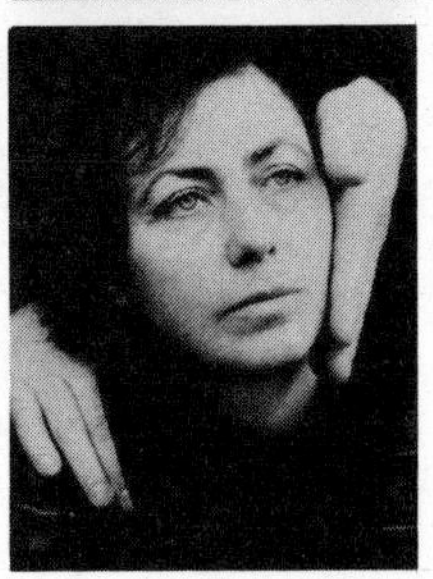

view. She wants to teach him Lars Gyllensten's ten commandments.

The Fourth Commandment: "Thou shalt take care of those who cannot take care of themselves."

BÖRJE: "Thou shalt take care of those who cannot take care of themselves."

LENA: The Seventh?

BÖRJE: The Seventh? What is that?

LENA: "Thou shalt, if you belong to the many who are better off than they deserve, share with others. Otherwise . . ."

BÖRJE: ". . . otherwise you are stealing." Who the hell is Gyllensten?

LENA: Lars Gyllensten is a fantastic guy.

BÖRJE: What's all this good for?

LENA: The old commandments weren't written for the

people of today. That's why he rewrote them.

BÖRJE: Mmm.

LENA: The First?

BÖRJE: "Thou shalt worship only temporary gods."

LENA: Mmm.

BÖRJE (*points*): What's that?

LENA: The school of Grönshult. With electricity and a well. Sold for 3000 kroner.

BÖRJE: That's damn cheap! Three thousand kroner.

LENA: Yes. People move to the towns. Mostly girls. They just can't live like they used to.

BÖRJE: No.

LENA: The Sixth Commandment?

BÖRJE: What's that?

LENA: "Thou shalt not spread venereal diseases, or bring unwanted children into the world, or expose other people to sexual violence. Also, you should play your part

in keeping the birthrate as low as possible, because altogether too many children are born. For the rest, you may devote yourself freely to sexual intercourse, masturbation, pornography and such other good things of this kind as your animal nature, in its grace, may cause you to desire."

The subject makes them both horny; Börje steps on the gas and off they go, driving through the beautiful old village of Övrakulla, now crowded with wrecked cars.

BÖRJE: And so, if he sells two or three cars a month, he'll make about 1200 kroner.

LENA: Mmm.

BÖRJE: Then you have the average guy who makes about . . . (*Börje looks around.*) What's this?

LENA: Two brothers sell junk here.

BÖRJE: Well, you see, the average guy earns 700 plus . . .

Then if he sells eight or nine cars . . . No, what the hell. He won't sell more than four or five cars, the average guy, that is . . .

LENA: Mmm.

BÖRJE: He'll make 1800 kroner a month. Yes, it's a tough business!

LENA: Mmm.

BÖRJE: Then you have the top guys!

LENA: Mmm. This is a typical dying village.

BÖRJE: Oh yes, it is.

LENA: Pity!

BÖRJE: Yes.

LENA: Do they cheat too, these guys?

BÖRJE: Between us, I can tell you that 1964 was a top year. That year a guy could make 20,000 kroner.

LENA: Twenty thousand?

BÖRJE: Twenty thousand a year. *Tax free!*

LENA: *Tax free!*

BÖRJE: But I guess a year like that won't come again.

LENA: Look! Look at the walls!

BÖRJE: Oh, yes.

LENA: To think that a hundred years ago they came here . . .

BÖRJE: Yes.

LENA: . . . and pushed and pulled . . .

BÖRJE: Yes.

LENA: . . . and slaved . . .

BÖRJE: Yes.

LENA: . . . to build these walls.

BÖRJE: Oh yes! Then . . .

LENA: And then they all moved away.

BÖRJE: That's right! Then you have . . .

LENA: It's really abandoned!

BÖRJE: Yeah!

LENA: Everything!

BÖRJE: Yes, but Lena, then you have the top salesmen! They make *45,000 a year!*

They park the car to wash it at a bend in the road where the Stångå has overflown its banks. Lena is emptying a little packet of car soap into the water.

LENA *(sings)*: "In Rio de Janeiro you can truck for free . . ."

Lena has poured the car soap into the river; Börje wets the sponge, Lena tries to open the trunk of the car. It is locked.

Can I have the key?

BÖRJE: I forgot it!

LENA: No, you didn't forget it, it's there on the key ring.

BÖRJE: I took it off and forgot it.

Lena tries on Börje's driving gloves.

LENA: How nice they are. But of course they should have been smaller and have had a big hole here.

With no apparent cause or explanation, she throws his gloves into the river. Börje is annoyed.

BÖRJE: Go and get them!

LENA: No.

BÖRJE: Get them!
LENA: No! *A-s-k M-a-r-i-e!*

With all their clothes on, they walk right out into the water. They throw the wet gloves at each other. Börje tackles Lena and both fall into the water and flail about. Börje grabs Lena.

How could you be so stupid as not to tell me about Marie?
BÖRJE: What?
LENA: You were stupid not to mention anything about Marie. If only you'd told me, it wouldn't have mattered. But going around keeping secrets like a damn . . .
BÖRJE: Like a what?
LENA: Are you going to marry her?
BÖRJE: I don't know. I don't think so. I have a child, you

know. We've talked a lot about it, Marie and I. It's a great responsibility to have a child. It's . . . I've thought a lot about it, but . . . No, I don't think I'll marry her.

They crawl into each other's arms, reconciled, and frolic in the water like a couple of otters, with only Börje's bottom showing.

They put their wet clothes on a line and drive through Rumskulla as if they'd just bought it. Singing "We shall overcome," Lena tacks one of her messages onto a tree.

MESSAGE TO HUMANITY:

I FEEL FINE NOW

—LENA

They are in the branches of an old oak tree, Rumskulla's main attraction.

LENA (*sounding like a guide*): The largest tree in Europe! Fourteen meters in circumference, 2000 years old.

Aroused by the sex education books she has been reading, Lena gets Börje's assistance in inventing an extraordinary, new (to date undiscovered and undescribed) position.

BÖRJE: What do you think?
LENA: Well, I guess it should work.
BÖRJE: Yes, I think so.
LENA: It isn't that bad, you know!

A cow appears briefly. On her forehead is a superimposed:

?

BÖRJE: No. Oh, hell, my thighs are aching.

A title is superimposed:

EXERCISE WITH TV

LENA: Your legs? They hurt?

They have separated. He unbuckles his belt.

BÖRJE: No, pain in my thighs.

LENA: Then you should feel the muscles I have! (*She removes her slacks and points to the "Musculus Protector Virgines."*) What do you think?

BÖRJE: What's wrong with them?

LENA: Here! Feel!

BÖRJE: Are they supposed to be like this?

LENA: No. It's because chicks squeeze their legs together.

BÖRJE (*as he simultaneously drops his trousers and shorts to his ankles*): Why?

LENA: They're not supposed to spread their legs like boys do, and that's how this muscle gets so hard. Then when they go to bed with a guy they can hardly spread their legs.

BÖRJE: But you don't have that problem, do you? You said you had slept with twenty-three guys.

LENA: Yes, but the first nineteen were no fun.

BÖRJE: Why?

LENA (*sighing*): I slept with them because they wanted to sleep with me, so that they could have orgasms. I couldn't believe that anybody could like me the way I look: with drooping breasts, big belly, fat.

In the middle of their highly confidential talk and tender embraces, they're interrupted by singing. A group of

fundamentalist Christians are having a revival meeting in the Sunday sunshine. They are singing: "He who created heaven and earth . . ."

27. Roses for Madeleine

They have returned to Lena's cottage after their sightseeing. Exhausted from lovemaking, they have fallen asleep on the floor naked. Lena awakens. Kneeling over Börje, she calls his name softly, checking to see if he is awake. Then she moves to his trousers, stealthily takes the key ring, and sneaks out to the car. She opens the trunk

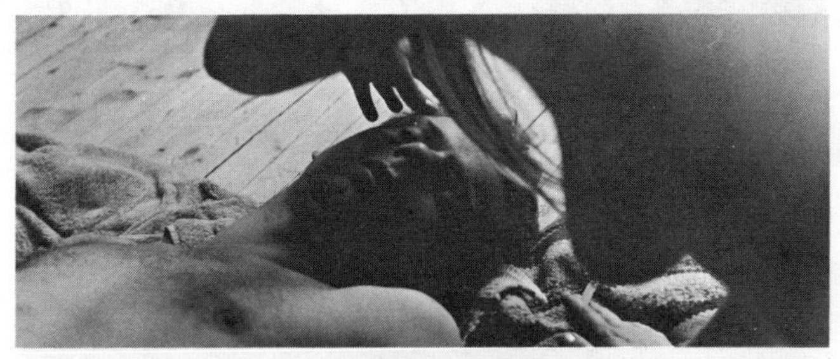

and finds a bouquet of half-wilted roses. And a hair dryer. Both apparently meant for someone named Madeleine—yet another of Börje's many girls. Lena reads the card.

LENA (*imagining what Madeleine might look like*): "Madeleine's wish is Börje's command."

Which is a hair dryer. A fine, new hair dryer. Bought

at a discount! Forty per cent off.

Lena sneaks back into the house, passing the poster of Gyllensten's Fourth Commandment:

THOU SHALT TAKE CARE OF THOSE
WHO CANNOT TAKE CARE OF THEMSELVES

She hides the hair dryer in the black bag—THE GUILTY

CONSCIENCE OF SOCIAL DEMOCRACY—*the contents of which the audience has been invited to guess.*

Titles appear on the screen as a reminder to the audience of the promises of the contest:

THE CABANA IN SPAIN
THE LUXURY CRUISE!
THE WINNER MIGHT BE
YOU

Börje lies half-awake on the floor. He calls for Lena. She enters silently, goes to Börje, crawls in front of him, her back to him. He pulls her to him, forces his way into her. She offers no resistance. Closed eyes. Violent movements. In the midst of their actions, she calls out questions as if conducting a public-opinion poll.

LENA: Does Madeleine have dark or blond hair?

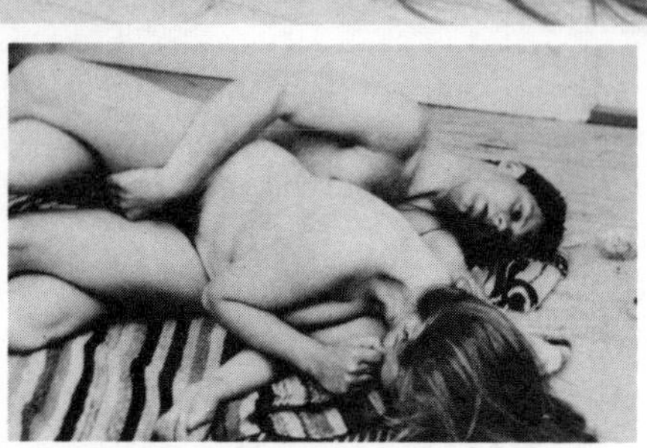

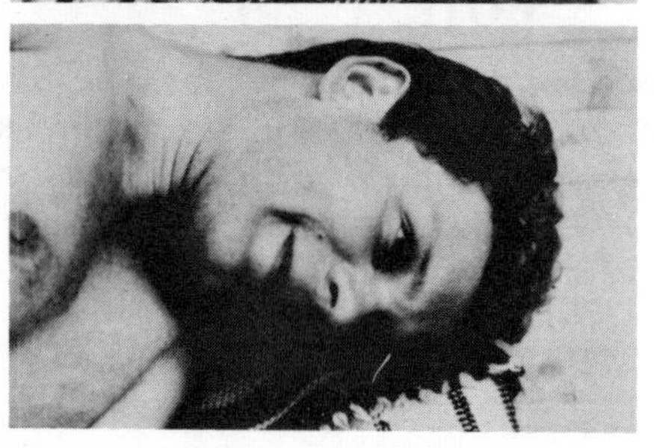

BÖRJE: Dark.
LENA: Which social class?
BÖRJE: Upper.
LENA: Fat or thin? (*She sticks her thumb in her mouth.*)
BÖRJE: Very thin.
LENA: The model type?
BÖRJE: Better than that.
LENA: Single?

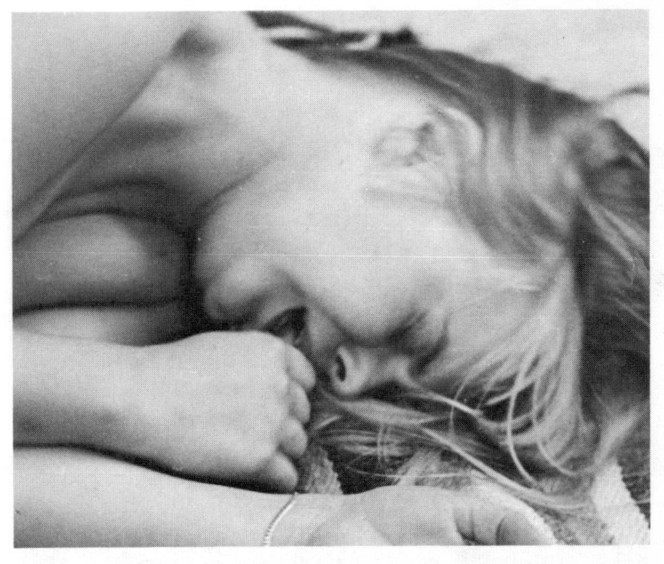

BÖRJE: Engaged. But she's going to break it off.
LENA: Because of you?
BÖRJE: Yes.
LENA: Did you know her before you met me?
BÖRJE: Yes.
LENA: Does she have better orgasms than I do?
BÖRJE: I don't know.
LENA: Haven't you slept with her?
BÖRJE: No, not yet.

Lena stops her questions for a while as they continue moving violently.

LENA (*screaming*): Why the hell haven't you done that?
BÖRJE: What?
LENA: Slept with her, of course! Why the hell haven't you slept with her?

She pulls away. Börje starts to get up. Seated facing each other, they continue.

BÖRJE (*shouting*): Damn your curiosity! You're always tearing everything into bits and pieces. Into talk and interviews!
LENA: Yes, and you're always keeping your mouth shut about everything! You told me nothing about Madeleine and nothing about Marie!
BÖRJE: You can easily put Marie or Madeleine in your files as well. Go ahead!
LENA: I don't want that upper class bitch.
BÖRJE: No, instead you want this kind of crap, don't you? (*He seizes the teddy bear she always takes with her and hurls it into the next room.*)
LENA: Keep your fucking hands off my doll, you pig.

She rushes into the next room, slamming the door behind her. She picks up her teddy bear, and runs, crying, to a corner of the room. Börje comes after her and picks up one of the books she had placed in a neat square around her typewriter.

BÖRJE: May I borrow this from you? May I borrow *The Passive Female Ideal?*

They struggle.

LENA: Yes, that's what you need. That's just what you have, a passive female ideal!
BÖRJE: What did you say I had?
LENA: A passive female ideal! Let go of me!

VAR HYGGLIG MEN INTE FLAT.
HAR DU SVÅRT ATT VÄLJA,
SÅ VAR HELLRE FLAT ÄN
STYGG.
GYLLENSTENS 8:e BUDORD

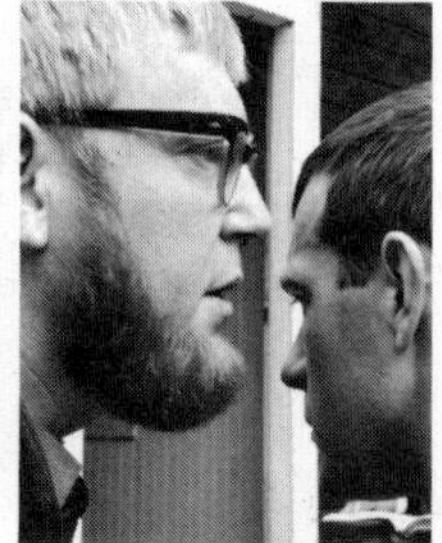

Lena dashes into the next room, Börje in pursuit. He grabs her by the elbows.

The film crew waits outside the house. Everyone tries to mind his own business, ignoring the unpleasantness within.

BÖRJE (*from inside*): Come here! Have a look!
LENA (*from inside*): That damn hair dryer! And the roses!

A door slams. Vilgot goes up to Raymond, the production manager, and asks him to close the outside door so that the racket cannot be heard.

Inside the house. Their screaming and struggling continues.

BÖRJE: Have a look around. Admit the fact that you're screwing around with things that are over your head.

It's all beyond you!

LENA: You lousy salesman!

BÖRJE: You've just got a big mess inside your head. Why don't you try doing something—like dieting? Why don't you put calorie charts on your walls instead of this stuff! And listen, you think you can ride in my MG with those drooping tits!?

LENA: You lousy salesman!!

She gives him a violent shove, knocking him over, and runs into the next room.

Börje gets up and runs after her. He grabs her, and they fall to the floor.

BÖRJE: "Börje's joy . . ." I'll give you a taste of "Börje's joy . . ."

She is sobbing as she lets him take her.

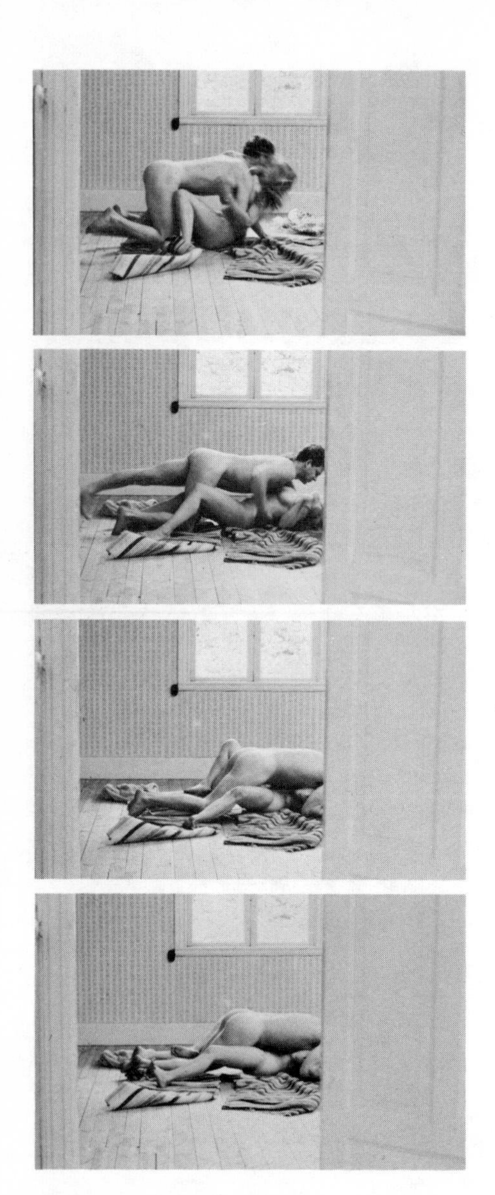

The sound of the car engine awakens her. She goes to the front door exhausted, only to watch Börje disappear in a cloud of dust. She stands for a time at the door, crying.

LENA (*voice over*): I didn't get much sleep the last night at Fagerdal. I was itching all over and everything was screaming in my brain. I remember one of the dreams:

how the Rumskulla football team came running through the woods. I got hold of them, both the varsity and the second string. But one of them was missing. There were only twenty-three.

Lena is tying the twenty-three boys with thick rope to another giant tree when the twenty-fourth comes through the woods. It is Börje. Lena grabs her rifle and shoots him down.

She goes to him, turns his dead body over, takes out her knife and castrates him.

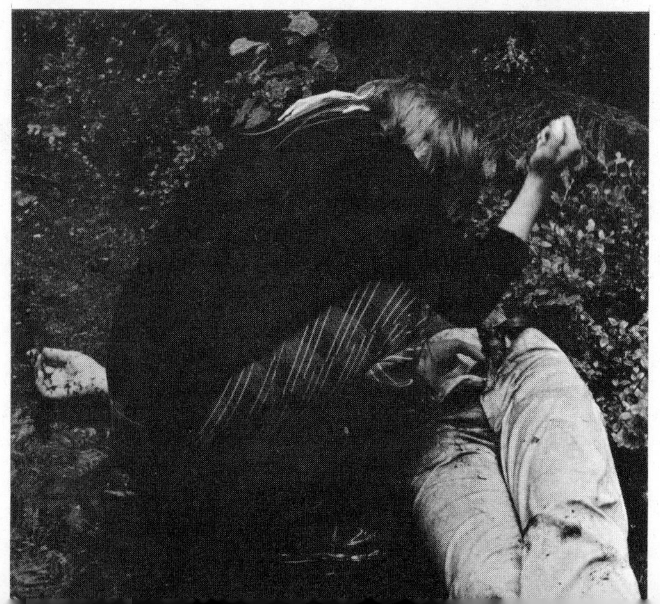

28. Lena's crisis

Lena's retreat is over. She leaves Småland. As she cycles back to Stockholm, several drivers offer her lifts. She rebuffs them with disgust.

Then she hears a fatherly voice calling to her.

VOICE: Lena! Lena! Lena! I want to talk to you. It's me, Martin Luther King.

She turns a deaf ear, but the voice continues. Finally she stops.

LENA: Listen, Martin! I'm terribly sorry that I just can't make it when it really matters, but that's the way it is. (*In despair.*) He's a big shit, that Börje! A big fucking shit and I'll *kill* him when I get hold of him.
I'll cut off his cock!

Martin Luther King gazes at her with insight and compassion. This is more than she can take. She closes her eyes; her lips begin to tremble.

You've said it yourself, haven't you? If you can't live by the principles of non-violence, you shouldn't be in on it! You've got to have people who are strong. (*Like a child.*) I'm never going to speak for your ideas any more!

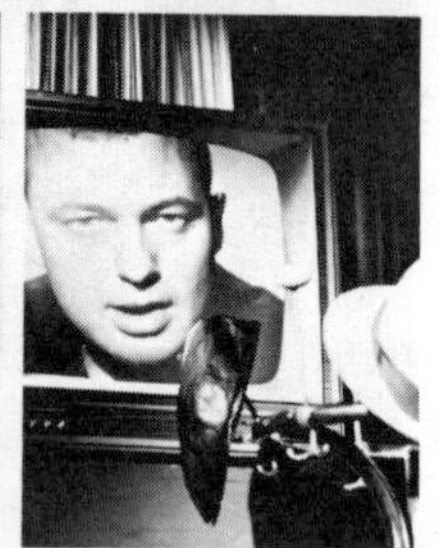

She is close to tears. She tries to comfort herself by going into a coffee shop. She breaks all the rules of her diet, stuffing herself on cake after cake.

Suddenly, a voice is heard from the shop's TV set.

BO HOLMSTRÖM: The long anticipated proclamation of the renewal of the Swedish defense system was issued at today's cabinet meeting.

The proclamation, which will be sent to all foreign countries, reads as follows: "The Swedish government hereby declares to the world that in case of enemy occupation of Swedish territory, resistance will be undertaken with any means except violence.

"The thorough instruction in non-violent techniques which all Swedish citizens, both men and women, have received over a long period of time enables us to carry out this method of defense certain that Sweden is uniquely equipped to meet any enemy attack."

Lena begins to cry uncontrollably. When she stops, there is a sense of relief. The idea continues, even if she has abandoned it. The idea is greater that she is.

The count on The Great Scandal Board increases from 11,328 to 11,330.

Lena cycles slowly into Stockholm.

29. An A-bomb for Sweden

A collection is being taken outside the Parliament building. A Swedish military officer is protesting official policy by standing with a collection box under a poster which reads:

GIVE YOUR SUPPORT TO A SWEDISH A-BOMB

He explains his viewpoint to people who stop.

OFFICER: As you know, Sweden is the only neutral country in Scandinavia, and to maintain our neutrality we consider it essential to have a deterrent weapon.

A MAN: Yes, but then all the other countries would start too. All Scandinavia would have bombs, and then, when the risk is that great, well, I mean, that could mean starting a war . . .

Lena cycles past.
Two Provos arrive. They are contemptuous.

FIRST PROVO: We'll give you a peace-button for support.

SECOND PROVO: A "Ban the Bomb" button.

FIRST PROVO: Here, move over so I can . . .

SECOND PROVO: Well, then, we've both put one in as a gift . . .

OFFICER: Thank you.

FIRST PROVO: . . . as a counter-demonstration to this terrible sign.

A third Provo appears and a Swedish worker sees the sign and stops.

WORKER (angrily): That's the worst goddam thing I've ever seen. Tear the sign down, you guys! What the hell, we're not going to have any atom bombs here, damn it all!

FIRST PROVO: To dare to present opinions like these, publicly! And in front of the Royal Palace, on top of

it all. Incredible!

The worker walks off, gesturing contemptuously.

Three nice little ladies who are very much in favor of the bomb open their purses as they look at the sign.

OFFICER: Well, we're polling Swedish public opinion.

LADY: Oh yes, I understand. Some sort of psychological test . . . (*She puts her contribution in the collection box.*)

OFFICER: Thank you.

30. Lena returns home

Lena has arrived home and is parking her bicycle in the backyard. As she is sticking a letter back on THE GUILTY CONSCIENCE OF SOCIAL DEMOCRACY *bag, a voice is heard reminding the audience of the big contest.*

SPEAKER: Oh, take it easy, Lena. It hurts. But where does it hurt the most? It's your opinion that we want. Yes, just yours! You who want a week of gymnastics with Princess Birgitta, your own cabana in Spain, or any of our innumerable consolation prizes. Nobody will leave our contest unrewarded, nobody who can guess what Lena found in the THE GUILTY CONSCIENCE OF SOCIAL DEMOC . . .

The speaker stops as Lena opens the door to Nyman's Institute and enters the kitchen. There on this bright

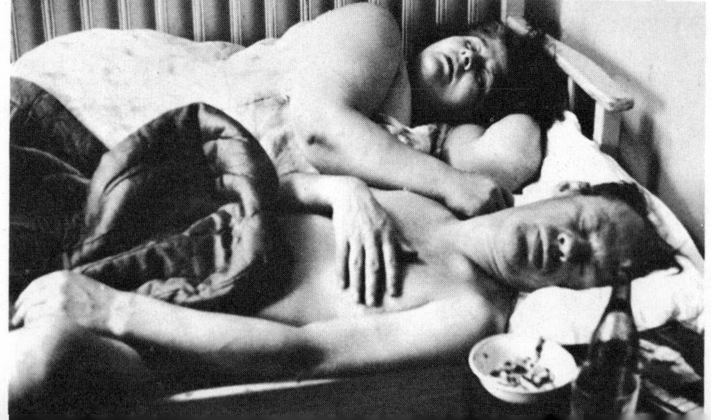

Sunday morning her father lies snoring. He is sleeping off a drunk. Beside him lies Chris, a big fat woman whom Lena hates.

Lena goes into her archive only to find that this has been invaded. There, lying on the floor, are a couple of her father's drinking buddies. Stricken, she leans against the fireplace and recalls how she used to attack the Great Injustice: "Some people were born with very little talent. They are lost, sort of butterfingered and brainless. . . ."

And now they're lying there, in her own archive, sleeping like little children. It reminds her of what Olof Palme said in his talk with Vilgot.

OLOF PALME: That's one thing: it is worse in most other places. But all societies have been tormented by the tendency to label people according to family, money, and social position. And we have this tendency here too.

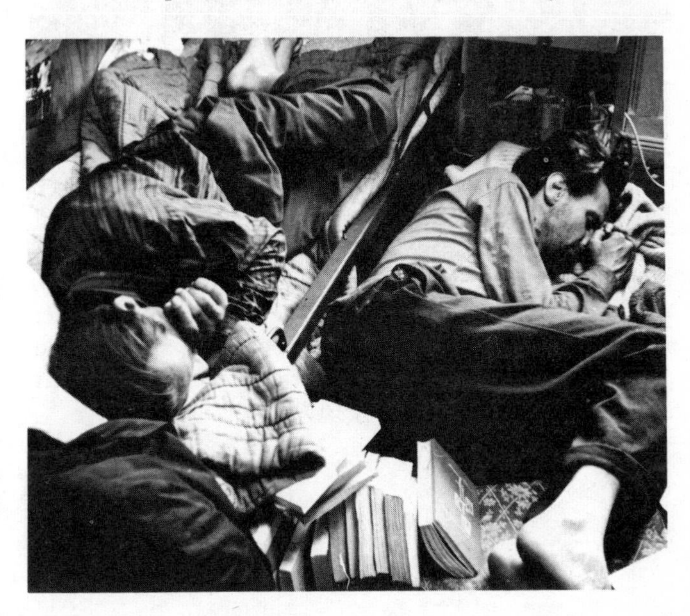

VILGOT: But there is an impression in other countries, I think, of great equality here, that we're far ahead in this area. What do you think?

OLOF PALME: Well, it's true that a lot of work has been done in that direction—partly on wages, and so on, but mostly we have worked on developing the possibilities for individuals. That's one thing: this enables us to know what direction to take in the future. But the other thing is that it's an illusion to believe that the trend toward equality has gone as far as some of the kinder critics of welfare states like to think.

31. British Motor Company

A foreign car showroom. Börje is dusting one of the cars on exhibit. He scratches at his fingers. Through the window, he sees Lena approaching. It is nearly closing time. Börje's boss comes out from his office onto the mezzanine.

BÖRJE'S BOSS: Börje! You sold the car to Mr. Johnson, I remember perfectly. Now he's on the phone and he's damned angry. I told you when you started selling cars that you can't just promise people the moon. You told him he'd get a radio and fog lights. You promised him practically everything you can put on a car, damn it. You can't do that. This is your last chance, next time you're fired. I'm so mad I could throw you out on the spot. This is incredible. It's not . . .

Börje scratches his neck. He can't think of a reply.

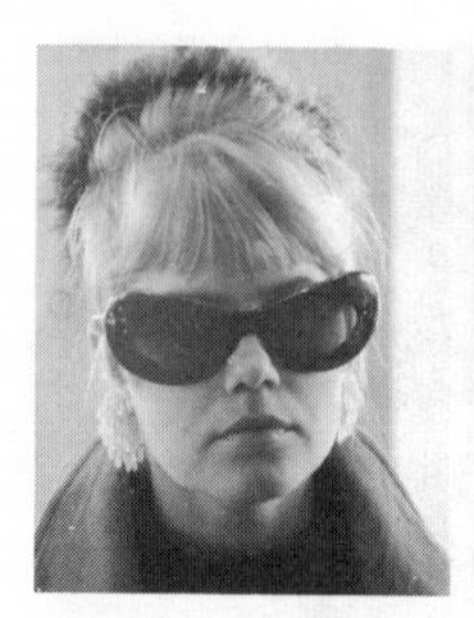

Then Lena strolls in carrying Madeleine's hair dryer.

LENA: Hello!

BÖRJE: Hello!

She hands him the hair dryer.

LENA: Can we go and talk somewhere?

BÖRJE: Yes, well I'm off now anyway. I could drive you some place. Shall we go down to the garage?

When they arrive at the garage, Lena helps Börje fold down the top of a white MG, a demonstration car. He tries to take her in his arms.

LENA: No! Have you been to bed with Madeleine yet? You have made some progress, haven't you? Of course it would be better if you hadn't, because I've got a case of scabies.

BÖRJE (*draws back*): So that's what I've got!

They don't get any further in this revenge scene, as Vilgot interrupts the shooting.

VILGOT: Cut! "From you" you were supposed to say. Didn't we agree to that? We're going to take it again!

A member of the crew absently begins singing: "I like the touch of fame, I like my own sweet name . . ." but is soon hushed. "Don't sing that *just now. Vilgot shouldn't*

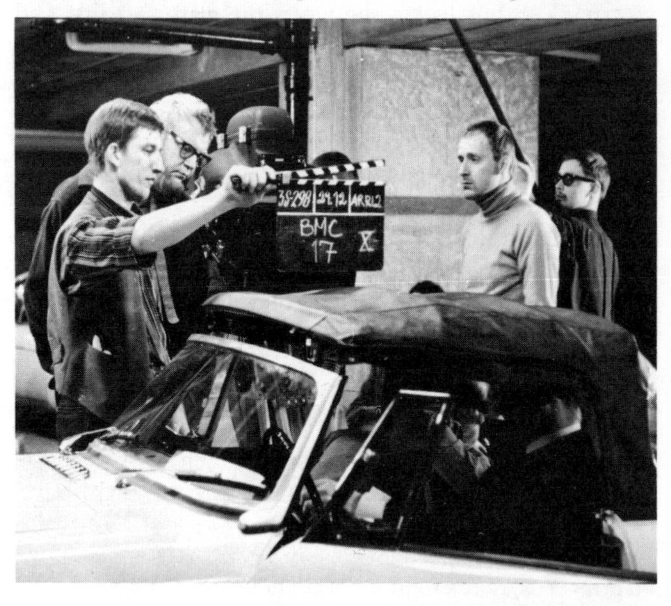

hear that." Looking hurt, the director watches the couple quietly talking to each other. They have obviously been intimate off camera, behind his back.

VILGOT (*voice over*): The damn girl is using me. She's using me like everybody else. This movie is her big break and she knows it, and God, does she ever take advantage of it! And along the way she takes Börje too. A toast to the Crown Prince! Skål! He doesn't really care about her, he just wants to compete with me.

Vilgot calls for quiet. They retake the scene. Again the director stops the shooting.

VILGOT: Well, excuse me a second. Lena, the glasses.

BÖRJE: What about them?

VILGOT: You should take them off when you begin talking . . .

BÖRJE: But she was supposed to wear the glasses during . . .

VILGOT: Yes, but listen, she wears the glasses at first and *then* she takes them off . . .

BÖRJE: What the hell, can't you make up your mind?

LENA: You changed your mind.

BÖRJE (*pointing to the script girl*): Ask Marianne.

VILGOT: I never changed that!

BÖRJE (*calling*): Marianne!

VILGOT: I said that from the start!

BÖRJE (*calling*): Marianne!

MARIANNE: Well, it *was* decided that she'd wear them.

BÖRJE: She should, yes.

MARIANNE (*to Vilgot*): Yes, Börje is right.

BÖRJE: See, I'm right.

VILGOT: No, no, you haven't understood a thing. She's supposed to wear them at first and then . . .

BÖRJE: Fourth take with, fifth take without, sixth with. Make up your mind, damn it!

Another take?

VILGOT: Yes, that's right, another take.

BÖRJE (*hostile*): Another take, huh?

VILGOT: Well, that's what we're here for.

BÖRJE: Yes, but make up your mind, tell us what to do. I'm listening. Lena and I are both listening!

VILGOT (*sarcastic*): That's fine. The Crown Prince is listening—until we're ready to shoot.

LENA: So I take them off?

VILGOT: Well, you start by having them on, you start by

talking about Madeleine, and then when you talk about the scabies you look into his eyes, see?

LENA (*sullenly*): Mmm.

VILGOT: And by then you've taken them off.

LENA: Mmm.

VILGOT: Is that all right?

LENA: Yes.

BÖRJE: Without glasses then?

Vilgot gives up. Those damned actors garble everything. Börje's boss and another B.M.C. salesman are standing in a corner, whispering. Vilgot walks over to them.

VILGOT: They're so scatterbrained, we're getting nowhere today . . .

BÖRJE'S BOSS: No, you can see that.

VILGOT (*a bit miffed*): What can you see?

BÖRJE'S BOSS: Well, this atmosphere is really shocking. How can you work under conditions like these?

Lena and Börge are whispering in the car. Lena is timid. Börje prods her.

BÖRJE: Have you talked to him?

LENA: No!

BÖRJE: Aren't you going to?

LENA: Yes.

BÖRJE: What?

LENA: Yes. Well, if he's going to be this way I might as well say it.

BÖRJE: Mmm. I think so.

LENA: Things can't get any worse!

BÖRJE: No!

Someone in the film crew begins whistling "The Internationale."

32. *Lena runs amuck*

The number 11,330 appears on The Great Scandal Board.

The same evening. Lena's father sits in his kitchen with his feet in a basin. Chris, the plump maternal female, fills it with hot water.

RUNE: Good!
CHRIS: Feel it now?
RUNE: Yes. A little more.
CHRIS: Little more. That's it!
RUNE: Mmm.
CHRIS: All right now?
RUNE: Mmm.
CHRIS: Good.
RUNE: Hey!
CHRIS: Mmm.
RUNE: He got his real gold frame.
CHRIS: Mmm.
RUNE: And you know how much it cost?
CHRIS: No.
RUNE: Two hundred and eighty kroner.
CHRIS: Oh, my goodness!
RUNE: Yes, and what's he going to do with it? Just sit there and point to it and say . . .
CHRIS: Hey!
RUNE: . . . to his guests . . . huh?
CHRIS: Wash your feet too!
RUNE: Yes, yes! Then he can tell his guests: "This frame cost two hundred and eighty kroner."
CHRIS: Well, so what? It's nice with a wide gold frame, and besides it's worth a lot.
RUNE: Yes, but listen! Do you think I've worked down there for half my life without knowing what art is worth? You know, the picture should be the important

thing and the frame should be less . . .

The door suddenly opens. Lena comes in.

What the hell!

Without a word, Lena goes straight to her archive. Her father and Chris look dumbfounded.

CHRIS: Has she come home? When did she get back?

Lena begins to empty her archive. She angrily brings out a carton and places it by the kitchen door. Chris gets angry too. She pours coffee.

Can't you at least say hello? That's the least one could ask.

Lena brings out another carton.

LENA (*accusingly*): Where's the collection of clippings on

Southeast Asia? I can't find it in there!

RUNE: Collection of . . . (*Rising.*) Hey, listen! Where the hell have you been all summer?

CHRIS: Nobody even dares stick his nose into your room with all the crap you have in there.

LENA: Oh, is that so?

CHRIS: That's right!

RUNE (*angrily*): Well, you should stay home and not run around on the roads and do . . . God knows what!

CHRIS: At least you could have sent a card to your father so that he'd know where you were. Don't you realize he's been worried?

LENA: He never has before.

Rune crosses to the sink and prepares to piss.

RUNE: And I've got to feel embarrassed in front of my friends at work because I don't know where my own daughter is.

LENA: That's none of their business.

RUNE: And Börje, he's been here looking for you.

The sound of Rune pissing. Chris pours another cup of coffee. Lena stalks into her room. Rune and Chris appear in the doorway.

Hey, are you going to leave home?

LENA: Home! You call this a home?

RUNE: Haven't I slept here in the kitchen? Haven't I done everything I could for you?

LENA: That's just your guilty conscience.

RUNE: Haven't you got the whole room to yourself? Haven't you?!

LENA (*in a fury*): That's just your guilty conscience! Do you remember at school? Remember that last day of school when you were there? That first and last time. God, was I ever ashamed! God, was I ashamed of you!

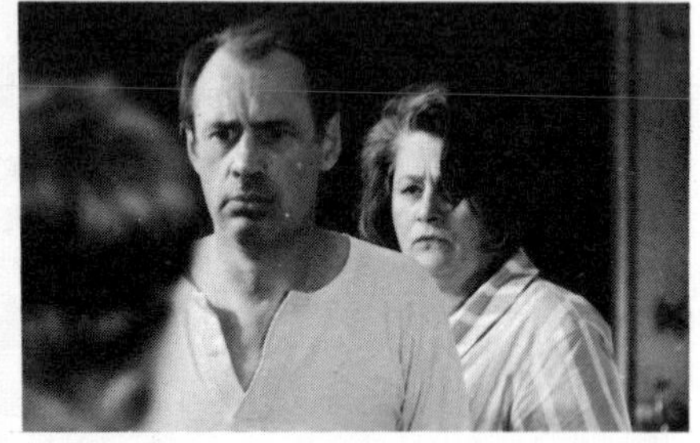

Do you think I could ever bring anybody home?! To this? You're crazy. You've done one good thing in your life. Do you know what that was? That's when you went to Spain. But why didn't you stay there? Why did you run home so quickly? Like a damned rat!

She slams the door, locks it, looks about, stops a second, and makes her decision. She pulls down the shelves, rips down the war photographs, throws down the books, and

tips over the bookcase. She destroys her entire archive.

CHRIS: What on earth is she doing?

She begins throwing empty beer bottles at the portrait of Franco. One hits and breaks the glass. The laurel wreath falls down. She takes two knives from the closet, raises them in measured ritual gestures, kissing them. Then she thrusts them one after the other into Franco's eyes.

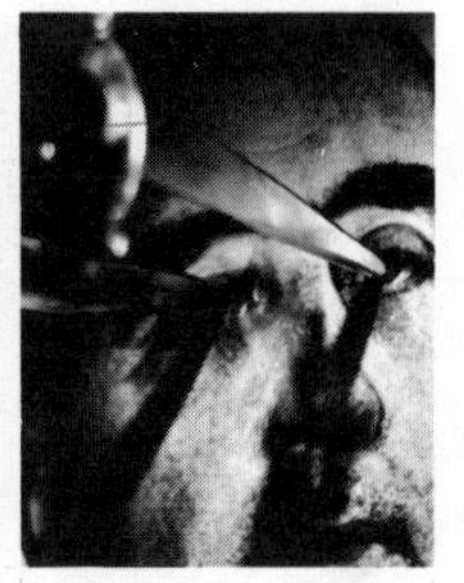

33. The cleansing bath

Saint George Hospital. The old bath house. The bath master is scrubbing Börje in a tub; a woman takes care of Lena.

BATH MASTER: Has it been itching a lot?
BÖRJE: What?
BATH MASTER: Has it been itching?

After the bath, their entire bodies, except for their heads, are painted with a DDT solution. They must wait twenty-four hours before washing it off. Then they are free from scabies.

The men's and women's sections are side by side. The film crew shoots them from a next-door room. Peter Wester, the head cameraman, checks the light while general assistant Bengt Palmers strums his guitar, looking for a tune.

BENGT PALMERS (*sings*):
"Lena, she stands in the tiled room,
she scratches her . . .
Yes, little friend, freedom is a hard thing.
Freedom is hard.
It tickled and itched between your legs
and now you're standing here
at the clinic at seven in the morning."

Lena stands naked. Börje stands naked. Vilgot leers at them. He seems satisfied as if he has his revenge by filming them in this situation. But he is content to turn to one of the women in the crew, Lena Malmsjö; he massages her shoulders.

BATH MASTER: Rub around . . .
BÖRJE: What?
BATH MASTER: Rub it into the pubic hairs!

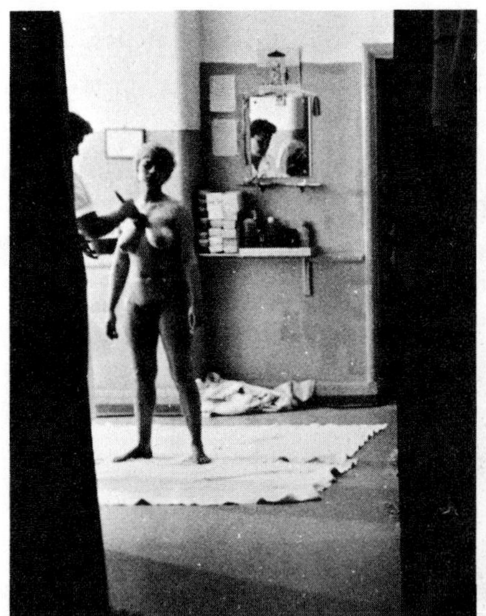
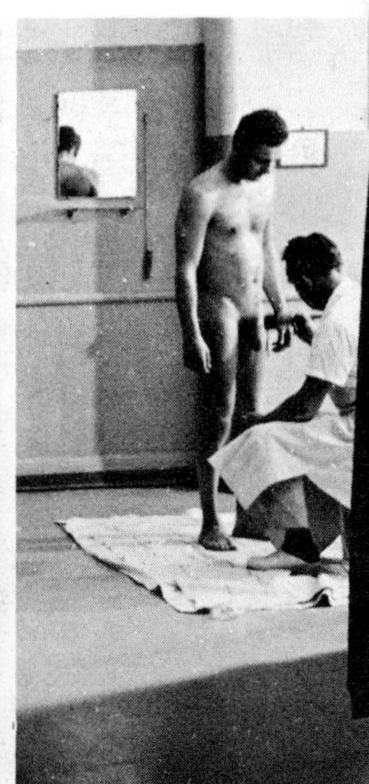
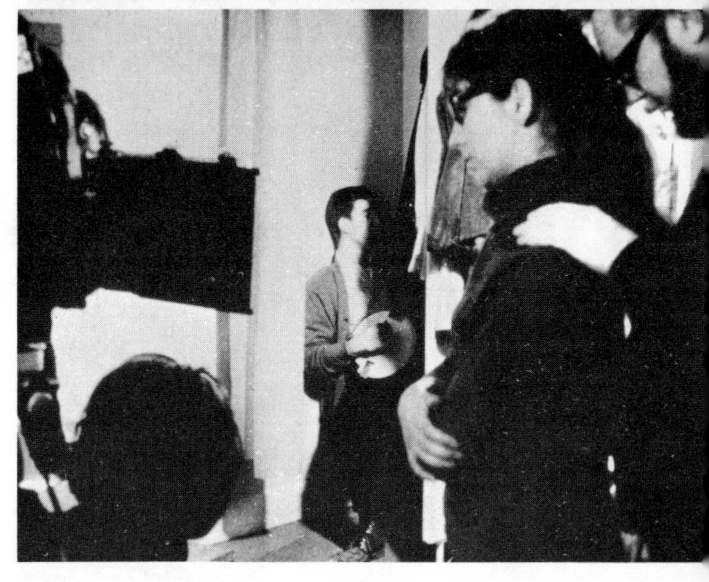

BENGT PALMERS (*sings*): "DDT stings and itches."

Lena and Börje leave the bath house. Outside the hospital they stop for a second.

BÖRJE: Can I take you somewhere?
LENA: No, I'm not going in your direction.
BÖRJE: Where are you going?
LENA: None of your business.

Bye-bye!
BÖRJE: Good-bye.

So ends the story of the car salesman and the girl with the archive. Each goes his own way.

34. At Sandrews

However, the story of the drama student and her film director ends differently.

A voice echoes through a loudspeaker down the corridors at Sandrews: "Olle Jacobson to the new sound stage . . ." "Bengt Ernryd to the music studio . . ." Director Vilgot Sjöman sits in the cutting room with MARIA SCHERER, DRAMA STUDENT, AGE 23.

He is running the rushes from the hospital for her, back and forth, and she is childishly delighted when he runs it at double speed making Lena and Börje sound like Donald Duck.

Lena Nyman comes down the corridor. Suddenly she stops. She has an unexpected attack of jealousy when she overhears Vilgot talking with a girl who seems to have the leading part in his next movie.

VILGOT: But, you see, you can't do anything in this country. It's just like a duck pond, everything stands still. It's just quack, quack, quack all the way.
MARIA SCHERER: No, no. Every Swede who goes to vote is full of ideas, but they never get a real chance to express . . .

His hand is on her shoulder.

VILGOT: Hey!
MARIA SCHERER: Yes?
VILGOT: You're cute when you get excited like that!

Maria smiles. Lena comes into the cutting room. Vilgot looks up. Maria Scherer looks inquiringly at her.

LENA: Hi!
VILGOT: You don't know each other, do you?
MARIA SCHERER: No. (*She introduces herself.*) Scherer.

LENA: Lena.
MARIA: What?
LENA: *Le-na!*
MARIA: Oh.

Lena hands Vilgot a key. It's the key to his apartment. She doesn't need it now that she doesn't live there any more. Vilgot takes it.

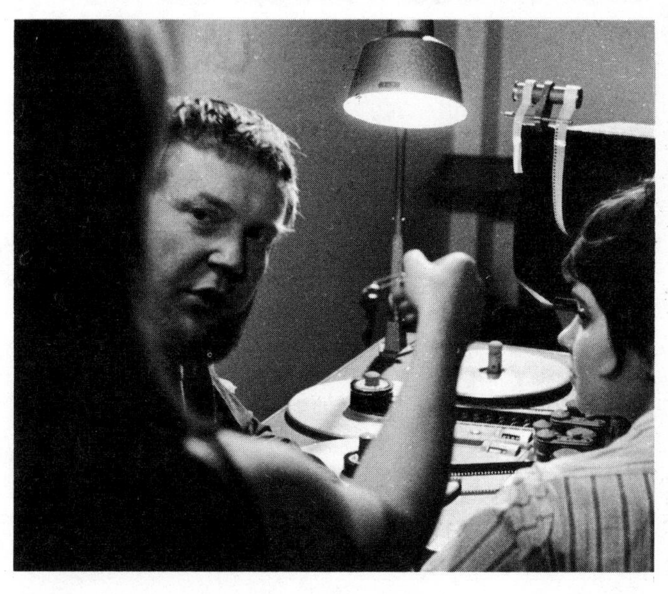

VILGOT (*tartly*): And the front-door key?

Lena has forgotten it.

Well, you can put it in an envelope and send it.

Outside, in the hall, Börje Ahlstedt, the actor, is waiting for Lena Nyman, the young drama student. In the elevator, they embrace, happy and free.

BÖRJE: What did he say? Was he difficult?
LENA (*takes a deep breath*): No. But God how glad I am that it's over!

35. Slogans

As the new lovers descend kissing in the elevator, the credits appear and slogans are heard again.

MALE VOICE: Buy our film! Buy it! The only film that comes in two editions. One is yellow and one is blue!
FEMALE VOICE: Buy the yellow! Buy the blue! Buy our film for there are two!
MALE VOICE: Exactly the same movie, yet each so different.
VOICES (*repeat*): This was the yellow edition. This was the yellow edition, etc.

The last image is a button with the slogan "Make love, not war" in English and the non-violent resistance emblem.

Director	Vilgot Sjöman
Cameraman	Peter Wester
Assistant	Andreas Bellis
Sound	Tage Sjöborg
Assistant	Christer Östberg
Editor	Wic Kjellin
Assistant	Wiveka Nordström
Script Girl	Marianne Johnson
Executive Producer	Lena Malmsjö
Production Manager	Raymond Lundberg
Assistants	Bengt Palmers
	Rudolf Adolfsson
Producer	Göran Lindgren

CAST:
LENA NYMAN
PETER LINDGREN (*Rune*)
BÖRJE AHLSTEDT
Magnus Nilsson
Chris Wahlström
Marie Göranzon
Ulla Lyttkens
Holger Löwenadler (*The King*)

Shooting took place in the summer of 1966, and in December/January 1966–67.

The Stockholm première took place on October 9, 1967.

Excerpts from the transcript of the trial

I Am Curious—Yellow, the film now playing in theaters in Sweden and Denmark, has run into serious censorship trouble in the United States, where U.S. Customs seized a print its distributor, Grove Press, attempted to bring into the country. Starring Lena Nyman, Börje Ahlstedt, and Peter Lindgren, *I Am Curious—Yellow* was approved unanimously by Swedish censors for showing without any cuts to anyone except children under the age of fifteen. One of the censors, Roland Haeggbom, called it "profoundly moral" and "very significant." Wherever the film has been shown in Europe, critics have acclaimed it as an important work of art with unusual relevance to contemporary issues and the social, political, and sexual problems faced by the young.

On May 20, 1968, before Federal Judge Thomas F. Murphy, a jury of seven men and five women convened in the U.S. District Court, Southern District of New York, to decide whether the adult public of the United States is to be denied a film which Scandinavian film audiences have flocked to see without any visible harm to the morals of their respective countries. For four days, the jury listened to a parade of witnesses testify to the social, political, artistic, and moral value of *I Am Curious—Yellow*. The witnesses appearing on behalf of the film included novelist Norman Mailer; Stanley Kauffmann, film critic of *The New Republic* and chairman of the National Society of Film Critics; Paul D. Zimmerman, film critic for *Newsweek*; John Simon, film critic for *The New Leader*; Hollis Alpert, film critic for the *Saturday Review*; the Rev. Dr. Howard Moody, Senior Minister of the Judson Memorial Church in New York City; Dr. Charles Winick, professor of sociology at the City College of New York; psychiatrists Dr. Edward J. Hornick and Dr. Thomas Levin; Ned Polsky, associate professor of sociology at the State University of New York in Stony Brook; and the director of the film, Vilgot Sjöman himself.

The Government, prosecuting the film on the charge of obscenity, presented only one witness, the Rev. Dr. Dan M. Potter, a clergyman in the forefront of numerous censorship drives. The jury, after deliberating for two hours, upheld the U.S. Customs ban and found the film to be obscene. The decision is currently being appealed.

The attorneys for the Government were Robert M. Morgenthau, United States Attorney for the Southern District of New York, and Lawrence W. Schilling, Assistant United States Attorney. The attorneys for Grove Press were Richard T. Gallen and Edward De Grazia.

One of the first witnesses was Stanley Kauffmann, who was examined by Mr. De Grazia.

Q. Would you state for the jury, please, some of the ways in which this film explores important issues of today?

A. I would begin by stating its basic tone, temper, or theme is the idea of transition, that the picture has grappled basically with the idea that we are living in a time of profound change in all aspects and perspectives of modern industrial civilization; and this basic theme of change, of transition, which is affecting all our lives, willy or nilly, is explored in four or five different veins.

That is, we see change in social attitudes, change in political attitudes, change in that version of political attitudes that deals with military views, changes in sexual relations, changes in the status of women in the society. . . .

Q. I wonder if you would please describe briefly and say a few words about each of the four or five themes of importance which you have isolated in this film.

A. Well, socially, we are dealing here with the emergence of the working class into what it hopes will be a classless society. The girl was the daughter of a working man, with some education, who is shown to us to be emerging from the formerly constricted and confined status of mind of a working-class girl that her mother's and father's friends are in, into a highly educated, inquiring state of mind. . . .

Politically, she is an activist, a radical. Insofar as her identities are formulated, she is very much in favor of radical political change. She is concerned about the political drift of her country; [of] the United States; equally concerned with disappointments in Russia, and it is made quite clear in the film.

Sexually, she refuses to accept any of the conventional bars that would have pertained, let us say, to her parents. She does this without, however, sacrificing, as is shown in the film, sacrificing any of her humanity or any of her consideration for herself as a person or of other people as persons.

In fact, the main inner personal conflict of the film is because she has been disregarded as a person by the man with whom she is having an affair in the course of the picture, because he has derogated her person by telling her a lie or by not telling her the complete truth about his situation.

The military theme I mentioned is perfectly clear. She wants Sweden to adopt a non-violent frame of mind toward future embroilments, and the director shows us a hypothetical kind of dream-wish-made-true of Sweden formally adopting such a non-violent program. We see a thing over television that we know is kind of a fabricated one. It is a wish non-fulfillment.

Psychologically, the film does its exploration in carrying forward at the same time several different strands of unassailable reality and of variations on that reality that play back and forth, that present a nicely variegated, thick texture of fact and sort of fantasies on fact, which is representative of what our society is beginning to be more and more aware of in terms of our daily perceptions of what we see, that there is a great difference between the black and white that has been formerly assumed of what is fact and what is fantasy. . . .

. . . In terms of some of the possible confusion that might arise in one viewing of the film, there is the basic technique that is used through the film of the director himself being in the film, and I understand that that is the director himself who plays the director in the film, and that the actress who plays the heroine is shown to be an intimate of the director, and that this parallel relationship between the director of the film and his friends runs alongside the relationship of the character she is playing in the film and the man she encounters in that regard. And this parallelism results in some confusion, which is only a confusion if you want things to be black and white.

Or another way of putting that is that what this director is aiming at is exactly that slight fuzziness, slight blurring of the line between what is fact and what is fiction.

It is part of a modern view of not just art but a lot of matters. What used to be thought of as a clear dividing line, an iron barrier between art and life, should go or can go or has gone, and we are not really aware of it yet.

And this film is an attempt to work in that field—to, in a sense, seduce us into believing in the reality of the fiction, then snapping us out of it into another reality outside of the frame of the picture. For example, in order to make us stop and think: "Well, what is real? What really is real?" For example, take the scene between the young man and the young woman in the car toward the end of the film. We have gone along with them in their relationship in the country and elsewhere, and we are pretty well absorbed in that relationship.

There they are in a car in a garage after she has gone to his automobile showroom and gone down into the neighboring garage with him. There we are with them involved in their story. All of a sudden, the director steps into the picture. The director of the film steps into the picture and tells them they are doing it wrong; they must do it over.

Now that, which is an unconventional thing to do in terms of our usual film-going experience, is a quite deliberate jar—shock—on his part, on the director's part, to bring us to with a start and say, "Well now, what is real?" We have been believing this scene between that man and that woman in the car, and all of a sudden he reminds us that that is a fictitious scene, and now we know that this is a fictitious scene, because this was rehearsed, that the director himself was going to step in, and he is trying to show us, I think, that what we have taken as absolutely fixed, concrete definitions of what is real in our minds have to be re-examined, that life is in truth a series of realities combined with unrealities.

And this film is particularly able to treat this question of what is real and what is unreal, for the obvious reason that the facility of shifting in and out, from one place to another, from one group to another and with real people, not like a novel, which leaves the reality of the people to your imagination. This device that he has used in this film is not original or unique. It has been used in a number of films in recent years—in the last three or four years at least—but it shows a growing interest, particularly on the part of younger directors, in this psychological question—philosophical question, really—of what we perceive, how we perceive it, and how do we know that it is really there. . . .

Q. Would you please give us your opinion concerning the interrelationships of the political and moral themes of this motion picture and the sexual scenes there?

A. Yes. I think the sexual behavior of the girl, as shown in this film, is perfectly consonant with her other states of mind as shown in this film. That is, it would be inconceivable to me that this girl would have the sexual standards of her mother or her grandmother, any more than she has their political standards, or any more than she accepts their social status as the man's slave—or "slave." That is one part of the sexual matters presented.

In other words, her behavior rings perfectly true. Her sexual behavior rings perfectly true to me for the character as shown.

There is another part of it, which is the showing of her sexual behavior in the film, and that to me rings equally true on a different plane, that is, a director, a film maker, was going to show the daring that this girl—showed the girl's daring in political and social and other matters. It seems to me he has to be equally consistent and bow no more to convention on the sexual scale than he does on any other, either of cinematic technique or political-social approach.

In cross-examination, Mr. Kauffmann was asked whether he held to the opinion that the director deliberately intended to break sexual taboos in making the film.

. . . I certainly do think that he was out to be as frank and permissive and radical in the sexual sphere as he was in every other sphere, so in that sense I certainly think he was out further, let us say, to widen the breach that had been made in sexual permissiveness in our time, yes.

Q. Is it your testimony, Mr. Kauffmann, then, that there

was an equal break with taboos in film-making in other areas in this film?

A. I think that the treatment of certain political subjects in this film is—It is very difficult to draw any kind of common scale in these matters, but it is certainly attended with the same frankness, the same wholeheartedness, the same modernity as he has treated sexual matters, yes. There is no sort of ruler or tape measure that can be applied to politics and to sexual matters, but, to put it this way, quite subjectively, the same mind, the same point of view, the same person made the sexual scenes as made the political scenes. That is quite clear.

The next witness was film critic Paul D. Zimmerman, of Newsweek, *who was examined by Mr. Gallen.*

Q. Would you please state whether you found this film to present ideas or themes of social importance?

A. Yes; a number of them.

Q. Would you please state what they are?

A. Well, what I thought was most valuable about the film coming into this country, as our own film industry does not look at the New Left, at the young New Left, which, whether you are for them or against them, is a very real element in our society; and this film, along with others at this time from abroad, looks at radical students, and the main, principal, subject of the film is a radical Swedish girl, whose political-social attitudes find their parallels in American young people. . . .

Q. Mr. Zimmerman, did you notice the theme of the breakdown of the family structure?

A. Well, I think it was made very clear in relationship with her father, and this brought in—to me it was interesting that it brought together both the political and the social question, what we call the generation gap in this country, that the father's experience in Spain, having deserted the anti-Franco forces, that this had lowered her estimation of him, and that has been a sore point between them, and that the political differences they have also create differences in the family. They don't communicate at all. They sort of mumble to each other. They have very little—It seems they have very little real contact, and I think this is true, this is happening as far as we can see in magazines and newspaper reports, this kind of breakdown over political issues as well as among others, happening in this country as well.

Q. What themes of social value in the picture did you find which have relevance to contemporary American society?

A. Well, the one that I just stated. I think the whole question of non-violence, which is particularly of interest to people of the heroine's age group—student or not student—in this country; the question of whether change can be effected non-violently, or the position of violence and non-violence in reform or in radical change. . . .

I think it is of interest to American audiences that there is much interest in the same questions in Sweden, that it is not simply an American dilemma, but it is one that has caused interest in all countries among this age, among others.

Q. In your opinion, Mr. Zimmerman, is the portrayal of the sexual scenes integrated and related to the main social themes of the picture?

A. Well, to elaborate on what Mr. Kauffmann said, I think that as well as being consistent with the outlook of the movie and with the outlook of the characters, I think that they also are useful in showing the relationship of the boy and girl. The sexual intercourse on the gate or on the wall in front of the King's palace—I think it is the King's palace—I'm not that familiar—I know it is an official building related to the royalty in Sweden—this is a gesture of defiance toward the old order. I mean, if anything embodies the old order, it is the royalty in the country.

And then, as she learns of the deception on the part of the hero or of her lover, the last sexual encounter, the one out in the sort of—the retreat, is rather brutal and loveless and unhappy, and the sexuality in a sense expresses the change in the love affair itself.

And I think that to make the kind of impact, to leave this to suggest—I don't see how a director could show this without being as explicit as the director has been. I mean, in other films, you can drift away at a certain moment and leave the audience to suppose what happens, but to show in sexual contact an expression of an attitude and a relationship, I think it has to be done explicitly, as it has been done.

Q. Is it then your opinion that there is artistic expression—artistic justification for the inclusion of the sexual scenes in the film?

A. Yes, yes. I think they are necessary.

The next witness, John Simon, film critic for The New Leader, *was examined by Mr. De Grazia.*

Q. Would you please tell us, first, whether you thought this film embodied or expressed themes or ideas of social or artistic importance?

A. Yes, I think it does.

Q. Would you please describe to the jury in your own way the most important themes, as you see it, in this film?

A. I find that to me the most interesting thing about the film is that it is a film that shows the interrelationships of various aspects of human activity, and of the society in which an individual human being lives. That is to say, it shows that there is no such thing as compartmentalization but that what a person is in his sexual relationships, in his so-called interpersonal relationships, in his family relationships, is related to his functioning as a citizen within the society in which he lives, and that this is a two-way relationship. What the personal relations of the individual human being develop in him is transmitted to that human being's relation to the entire society, and, conversely, the way the society functions or malfunctions is also transmitted to the individual who lives in that society.

To become fully aware of this two-way relationship is an important thing, to me.

Q. What do you think is the meaning of the title of the film?

A. I think it expressed the natural, and I think healthy, curiosity of today's young people to find out more about the actualities and potentialities of their lives, of what they can do with themselves, of what they can do for the world they live in, and what they can do for their nation, for their society—for the world, in fact. . . .

I find that Vilgot Sjöman, the director, has done something very fine in that he has shown uniquely in the film the different types of film-making—different ways of telling the story feed into each other. He uses a technique called *cinema verité,* which, as you may know, is film journalism. It is a kind of candid camera reportage, interviewing people in streets and public buildings, and so forth, about their opinions. This is a technique that has been much used by modern film makers. But usually, usually a whole film is dedicated to this technique.

The way Sjöman has made his film partly this and partly a story film is another way of saying, I think, that reality—or as much reality as you can literally put on screen—is not to be compartmentalized away from fiction, from imaginative artistic viewing and rendering of life, but that the two can flow into each other, and that the so-called story and the so-called journalistic part of the film really interdepend.

And in many other ways he has shown the introduction of one thing into another in what I think is a realistic and to my mind quite original way.

Q. You mentioned earlier, I believe, that this film interestingly connected one's sexual life with one's political life. Is this common to American films?

A. No. I think we have more—Those of us who take films seriously are more forced to admit that we must depend on European films for our spiritual and intellectual sustenance rather than on American films. This is regrettable, and I hope it will not always be so, but as of now it is European films that really address themselves to what I consider the important issues in life, whereas Hollywood films especially, but American films in general, tend to be much more glossy, superficial, formula-oriented, and less willing to probe and maturely consider psychological and social and political issues. To me it is the novelty and contribution of this film, along with many other European films, that it shows a human being from all angles rather than from a narrow, arbitrary, limiting sort of point of view which serves only getting the story ahead—and the story being just the plot—without any deeper human significance. . . .

It shows that when sexuality functions well between two people, this produces a kind of hopefulness about the society, and an enthusiasm; and inversely, when the girl herein, Lena, is feeling good about Swedish society, even to the point where she imagines that non-violence has become the order of the day, her private life functions better, more happily, and her sexual intercourse is stimulating and life-giving and happy and healthy, but that when she discovers the deception of her lover, and when, consequently, their relationship becomes troubled and unhappy and painful, she finds that her ability to function as an inquiring reporter, as a worker for peace, as a champion of non-violence, is also impaired by the fact that her physical fulfillment has been damaged and lessened.

Q. How would you say the treatment in this film of contemporary political issues compares with the treatment of political issues in the typical American film?

A. Well, I think it is more honest, I think it is more inquiring; it is more far-sighted, far-reaching; it is more adult.

Q. And how would you say the treatment in this film of sexual attitudes and activity compares with the treatment in the average American film?

A. I think this is one of the—I would unhesitatingly use the word "noble"—one of the noble things about this film, that it is unflinching, that what it has to tell it tells rather than pussyfooting up to it and around it. It does not leer, it does not smirk, it does not hint, it does not make prurient suggestions. It tells its story forthrightly and candidly without, I think, any excessive dwelling on anything except on what it considers vital and relevant. And I again agree with the previous testimony, earlier, that there are three or four films, for example, now to be seen on our screens in which such things as oral intercourse are hinted at in a distinctly suggestive way, but by the very fact that they make it on the one hand very plain what is going on, but on the other hand they don't have the courage to make it unmistakable, I feel that they portray a kind of dishonesty, a kind of Jesuiticalness which I think is an unattractive aspect of a work of art, whereas candor and facing the issues squarely I consider an artistically courageous and honest and salutary thing.

Q. Are there other films that you know about and have seen exhibited in the United States which in their sexual aspects go as far as the sexual scenes of this film?

A. Well, in the explicit sense they don't go as far, but I think a film that implies a great deal might in some senses be said to go farther and farther in the direction of confusion, nasty insinuation, encouraging the viewer to fantasize and possibly supply indeed quite illicit things, where spelling out something might almost be said to my mind to be going less far, if by "going far" we mean overstepping some kind of sensible, healthy, sensible kind of boundary. If by "going far" we mean going far in the direction of honesty and attempt to understand, then this one goes quite a bit farther. . . .

Q. There was, however, a scene, wasn't there? do you recollect a scene where Lena was kissing her boyfriend's genitals?

A. Yes.

Q. Would you give us your opinion on the intention and meaning of this scene?

A. This scene to me shows a rather touching rapport between the two sexual partners at that moment, and it is an interesting scene because—well, first of all, let me say what it immediately does, and then what it implies. It shows that at a moment of sexual fulfillment which in this case apparently involved oral sex, the two partners in love—Lena and the young man—are made very happy by this, and feel a kind of devotion and dedication for each other, a freedom of each other, a bodily freedom as well as an inner freedom, so that their entire bodies became objects of reverence and gratitude, and I very strongly felt that in the kiss delivered by Lena to her lover's genitals she expressed a very touching, a very human, a very childlike, sweet and simple devotion and gratitude to him for the happiness, for the joy, he has given her. And it showed that this kind of, perhaps unconventional, I don't know, sexual relationship is in fact a fulfilling and a sustaining and a devotion-making relationship.

Now, what was then particularly interesting is that this

happened during a phase of their relationship when things were already going downhill, and when the fact that her lover had lied to her, plus her growing realization that non-violence was not really consistent with her spiritual abilities, has already cast a shadow on the relationship and on her self-awareness, and I think the implication is that even in such a situation, temporarily physical well-being can act as a cementing and positive factor.

But it also shows, I think, that ultimately this is not quite sufficient, and that when the psychological and moral aspects of the relationship are failing, are no longer satisfactory, that the physical satisfaction can be only a partial and a temporary and transient relief and release, an oasis in the relationship. . . .

Q. In the respects, Mr. Simon, that you have just related, that you thought the film went further than any other films in the sexual area, I just wanted the record to be clear. In those respects did you think this film was a better film and was important by comparison with the average film which is seen in this country? Would you couch your answer in terms of importance?

A. Yes, I think that in whatever respects it can be said to break new ground I feel that it makes a genuine artistic and moral contribution by being honest about sex, by showing the enjoyment to be derived from it as well as the problems it raises, by showing its relationship to other aspects of the human personality, and the social and even political situation of the world, and by trying to understand the human being from all its sides rather than as is customary from just one or two sides.

Hollis Alpert, film critic for the Saturday Review, *was examined next by Mr. De Grazia.*

Q. Would you say the sexual themes involved in this film have any importance, social importance?

A. It is my feeling that the characters in the film, notably the young girl Lena and the boy, are exploring sex to an extent in terms of, let's say a more honest approach than was true of previous generations. . . .

Q. Is the quality of honesty a matter of importance in this film?

A. I think it is of very great importance in this film, which is one of the reasons why I am here to talk about it. I have been concerned, as have many other critics, with dishonesty in portrayal of sex and sexual relationships over a great many years. I think this is one of the very few which has dealt with the theme and the subject with great candor and honesty and, to a certain extent, artistry. I find it a very important film, indeed, for that reason. . . .

The Reverend Howard Moody, Senior Minister of the Judson Memorial Church in New York City, discussed what he felt was the religious dimension of the film. He was questioned by Mr. De Grazia.

. . . Martin Luther once said that man's God is whatever he hangs his heart on, whatever he deeply believes in and is committed to, a kind of ultimate allegiance.

[This] film is sort of an exposure of the gods of the Swedish young people: Yoga, non-violence, sexual emancipation, freedom for all, class structure. All of these were an exposure of these beliefs and commitments of the young. And I think that whenever a film deals with this kind of subject in an open and honest way, it has a very significant religious dimension.

A religious film is not only one about theological subjects. A religious film is one that deals with the choices and the problems of human action and says something as a work of art about those choices.

Q. Then is it your opinion, Dr. Moody, that this film is a film of religious importance?

A. Yes. I think it is of religious import and of very important socio-cultural import.

I might say a word about the sex in the film, which is one aspect of it. I do not consider it the major aspect of it, but it is one theme amongst many themes in that film.

I might say that I believe that according to religious teaching, that sex is a sanctified part of human nature, but it is not sacrosanct. I might say what I mean by that. By being sanctified, sex is believed by the Creator as part and parcel of the human condition and made for the enjoyment and perpetuation of the species.

We have made it, I think, sacrosanct, that is, sacred in kind of a set-aside way, untouchable, more than human.

The human sex in that film, I believe, from my own perspective, was not perverse, it was not sadistic, it was not violent; but it was straightforwardly human sex, and I might say parenthetically, from my own perspective, rather healthily heterosexual, which I deeply appreciated.

Q. Did you notice political themes in this film which in your opinion were of importance for contemporary American society?

A. I would say that very important moral and political questions are raised in that film. . . . I must say at this point—I have to say—most political questions from my own perspective, and from a lot of religious perspectives, are moral at base. When we raise a question about human actions, their collection together, their being governed, the ways in which they are governed, the ways in which they are fed and clothed, all of these things—the way they are looked at and treated, the amount of freedom and responsibility that is required of them by political forces, are basic moral questions from my own perspective; and I believe that film was full of them and raising some very significant questions in that instance about Swedish life. I think most of us know that those same questions are familiar in American life. . . .

Certainly, the basic theme of the film, the one on which he hung the film, was the question of class structure in Sweden, and there was exposed all the prejudice and ignorance of the Swedish people regarding their own nation and the way it was governed, and so forth.

And I suppose one could translate it today in terms of America as to whether racism is something that exists, in the kind of probing and questioning that the film did. It is entirely relevant to our own situation, I think. . . .

. . . perhaps the dirtiest picture in the world was not the picture of a man and a woman making love but the picture of the piled-up corpses at Buchenwald and Dachau; this was far more obscene and did more, far more, violence to the human situation, human action, than all our slick-paper graphic essays on sex, the human body, and so forth.

There is nothing obscene or dirty about the human body, but there is about men's violent treatment of that body, and this I felt was the real obscenity. . . .

On redirect examination by Mr. De Grazia:

Q. Dr. Moody, would you care, please, to explain your responses to the questions asked of you by the Government counsel concerning the sanctified sexual aspects of the scenes that he asked you about?

A. Well, I would simply say, because when I used the word "sanctified" for people I try to put a particular definition on it, namely, that it was a part of the creation believed by the Creator and given as part and parcel of the human condition and the human situation for the enjoyment and perpetuation of the human species; and that is what I mean by "sanctified."

And when you ask me if the sex in that movie is sanctified, I mean by that that it is normal and healthy in the way in which sex has been given to us in this world. That is what I wanted to say. I mean, I am not one to say that I believe that sex—I don't believe in sexual exhibitionism, and the question as put to me was not what was right or wrong, whether it was right or wrong to engage in sex on the balustrade of a government building. We haven't very much of that. It is a figurative way of saying something about the government, I think, which I won't try to vocalize.

I think it was another kind of statement in the film.

Q. In other words, the balcony or the balustrade scene involves Lena and her boyfriend in expressing a point of view about the authority of the government or the palace?

A. Yes, I do.

THE COURT: What point of view were they expressing, in your opinion?

THE WITNESS: Well, I would say they were saying, in a sense, "Screw the Government." That's what it seems to me they said.

Dr. Charles Winick, licensed psychologist, professor of sociology at CCNY, and from 1961 to 1967 a consultant on censorship standards at NBC, was questioned by Mr. Gallen.

Q. Could you tell the jury what conclusions you have reached concerning the changing standards in the movies concerning the expression of sex?

A. I think that when I did the report on *Taste and the Censor* [*on Television*, published by the Fund for the Republic, 1959] ten years ago, there was no doubt that the theater was the most liberal art form in terms of its ability to express sexual material, and it was pretty much on a par with novels.

I think, however, that in the last two or three years there has been a substantial change here, and movies, which were about ten years behind novels and the theater, now are accepted by Americans as expressing relatively liberal material that previously would not have been acceptable in a movie.

I think that young people especially look to movies for new ideas and new material, and they are willing to accept sexual content they may not have been able to accept before, and since over fifty percent of the movie audience in America today consists of young people between the ages of sixteen and twenty-four, I think that the expression of sexual material is of special interest to these young people who are trying to find themselves and who look to a movie not just for entertainment but for clues to understanding the world they live in, and increasingly they find such clues in movies like the British *Blow-Up* or the Yugoslav film *Love Affair* or the Danish film *I, A Woman*, all of which have been released in the last year or so and all of which show nudity, sexual relationships presented quite openly, outside of a marital situation and so forth.

And I think that this is part of the satisfaction that these films provide, that they deal with sexual material in an interesting way, and they not only have an entertainment value, but they enable these young people to perhaps understand a problem that they have.

I would summarize by saying that in the last five years and notably in the last two years, movies have moved to the forefront in terms of the performing arts in the freedom with which they present sexual material and, more importantly, to the extent to which their audiences anticipate that they will see sexual material presented in a relatively frank manner in films.

Q. In your opinion, does the presentation of the sexual material in *I Am Curious* exceed the expression of sexual material in other films that you have seen during the past three or four years?

A. No. I would say that it is more or less on a par with the films that I mentioned. Perhaps the oral-genital scenes have not been presented quite so openly in these other films, but in terms of the larger context of the film, I think that this film, *I Am Curious,* is on the same level as those I have mentioned, which have been shown successfully and which are now taken for granted.

Q. In the course of your studies, have you become familiar with the expression of sex in novels or books?

A. Yes; I have.

Q. What is your opinion with respect to the expression of sex in novels and books as compared to the expression of sex in *I Am Curious?*

A. I would say that some best-selling novels present sexual material frankly, like James Purdy's *Cabot Wright Returns* [sic], Ken Kesey's *One Flew Over the Cuckoo's Nest,* and *An American Dream* by Norman Mailer, the *Beautiful Losers* by Leonard Cohen, and *City of Night* by John Rechy. These are all best-selling books published in the last few years.

I would say that the presentation of sex in *I Am Curious* is perhaps slightly behind the presentation in these well-known novels that I have mentioned, in that it is perhaps less—even less explicit than in the novels.

Q. Dr. Winick, were you asked to testify on behalf of the Government in this case?

A. Yes. I saw the film at the invitation of the Government, I think, on March 7th.

Q. And what did you tell them?

A. That after seeing the film I did not feel that it was obscene and therefore I could not testify to that effect. . . .

During the cross-examination by Mr. Schilling:

THE COURT: The question was, Doctor, would you explain the connection between the sexual intercourse in the tree, or on the tree, with the other problems that this girl had?

A. The choice of this tree I construed to be an expression of defiance of authority, which is one of the major themes of the film, by selecting what appears to be an otherwise bizarre locale for sexual activity.

Q. By "defiance of authority," what authority are you referring to?

A. Well, since part of the—since a major theme of the play is the girl's exploration of herself and her exploration of various aspects of Swedish society, this venerable tree, it seems to me, is a symbol of age and something that is very substantial, and since we do not ordinarily expect people to engage in sexual intercourse in a tree, this is an additional expression of defiance.

THE COURT: The question was, defiance of what?

THE WITNESS: Defiance of authority, what is represented by her father, by the Swedish Government, the Minister of Information* she talks to, and the King—in other words, the whole organized social structure of Sweden is kind of symbolically presented, symbolically represented by the tree. . . .

Q. Do you recall any scenes of cunnilingus or fellatio in the film?

A. Yes.

Q. Will you explain the difference between those scenes in the film and the social and political issues?

MR. GALLEN: The prior question had a conclusion of law in it, and it was answered before I could object. There is no cunnilingus or fellatio in the movie, and Mr.

*Actually, the Minister of Transportation, Olaf Palme.—*Eds.*

Schilling is aware of this point, because it was pointed out to him on the pre-trial depositions.

THE COURT: Whether he is aware of it or not aware of it, it is a question of fact for the jury.

I might tell the jury now to disregard the statements of counsel. It is their recollection which controls.

I will permit the question.

A. Well . . . just prior to the oral scene, the girl is involved in this episode with the non-violence, the altar and the material with Martin Luther King, and it seems to me that the director here is communicating by the use of oro-genitality—he is communicating in a contrapuntal way the element of non-violence.

In other words, morality is essentially a form of sexual behavior which is not aggressive in the traditional sense. That is, it is a form of sexual relationship which is passive on the part of at least one of the partners, and the director is juxtaposing two things.

Just as in her desire to meditate and explore fully the implications of non-violence in social life—Martin Luther King, the broken gun, et cetera—immediately thereafter we are shown the girl engaged in a sexual relationship which is also, in effect, non-violent and passive. And it seems to me the director is consistently trying to show us the relationship between orality of various kinds and passivity.

Thus, her father, who was a failure, has become a drunkard. He drinks, an oral person. Then, when the girl is disappointed, she stuffs cakes into her mouth in the drugstore. I think the director brings together these two things in a very provocative way, and each one helps to clarify the other. The orality, both on the part of the male and on the part of the female, coming just as it does, after the concentrated material on passivity, it seems to me, shows how in her personal life, even in sexual behavior, it is possible for her to be passive—in other words, non-aggressive—just as she tries to do this in her social life and in behalf of the cause in which she is interested.

Q. You testified that this film, *I Am Curious*, is more or less on a par with other films being exhibited insofar as its sexual scenes are concerned. Is that correct?

A. Yes; I would say so.

Q. Have you ever seen any other commercial feature motion-picture film that had an equal emphasis on male nudity, the male genitals, female nudity, and the female genitals?

A. A number of the Andy Warhol films have extended scenes of nudity in male and female—with male and female genitals.

Q. You would consider that was with equal emphasis?

A. No, because there the director doesn't seem to have the same kind of social and political commitment that this director seems to me to have.

Q. And are those films that you have referred to, if you know, films that are exhibited nationally in theaters?

3. *Chelsea Girls* has been shown in dozens of cities and been enormously successful, for example—the Andy Warhol film.

THE COURT: I don't get the word—

THE WITNESS: Andy Warhol.

Q. Can you think of any other films which have the equivalent amount of emphasis on male and female nudity?

A. Well, I think it is necessary to take the overall intent and theme of the film. It is not really meaningful to take the amount of time devoted to nudity or sexuality and make judgments from that.

Q. Whether it is meaningful or not, I would appreciate an answer to the question.

A. Certainly. Several of the Andy Warhol films, such as

the *Chelsea Girls* and a film like *I, A Woman* and *Love Affair* have perhaps as much, I would say, proportionately, nudity and non-marital sex and sex of a kind that is not traditional.

Q. You say perhaps as much, and you mentioned things other than nudity. Again, I would appreciate an answer to the question.

A. Well, addressing myself to nudity and sexuality, I would say that *I, A Woman* and *Love Affair* have approximately as much sexuality and nudity.

MR. SCHILLING: Your Honor, I ask that that answer be stricken as unresponsive. My question dealt with the emphasis on male and female nudity and on the male and female genitals.

THE COURT: I think he answered the question.

Q. Is there any commercial feature motion-picture film that devotes as much time to scenes of sexual intercourse as *I Am Curious*?

A. No; I don't think so.

Q. Is there any feature commercial film that deals with sexual intercourse with the explicitness and to the extent that *I Am Curious* does?

A. Well, the Andy Warhol films present Lesbian intercourse, homosexual intercourse, in great detail and on camera for much longer periods of time, and I think that the very explicitness of the sexual scenes in this film actually is relatively healthy, because we do not have to imagine what is happening and, therefore, the film is relatively unlikely to, it seems to me, to inspire people to fantasize, because it is so literal, whereas another film, where there might be a fade-out of a couple in bed, and then a shot of waves breaking and a window shade being pulled down—this is the sort of thing that would in fact inspire fantasies.

But in this film, the very literalness, it would seem to

me, would serve to quell fantasies that people might have. . . .

Dr. Edward Hornick, psychiatrist, was examined by Mr. Gallen.

Q. Doctor, in your opinion are the sexual scenes of the film related to the development of the main political and social themes of the film?

A. I think they are in this way: I think we come from a romantic background in the Western world where we so often think of the difficulties of growing up into the hazards of adult living in our social system, in our political system, in the hard competitive world outside that are mediated through sexual love. I think this is an ideal entered into by many, if not most, of us, that we find we are able to make a go of living as adults because there is some one person whom we love and who loves us, and that thereby we can face the difficult realities of, to put it kindly, not so good political systems, not so honorable social systems. But because somebody loves us, and we love somebody, we can find a meaning and a close personal family life level that makes sense to us.

It seems to me that we see in this girl tortured and torn as she is coming from this terribly broken home and striving for women's rights, and striving for the rights of the underdog, striving for the lower classes, really a striving for herself which she hopes to achieve through her sexual union which she hopes will eventuate in a marital union.

As you know, the thing that knocks this entire picture into a cocked hat is her discovery that the man not only has another girl friend, but has another girl friend and a child by the other girl friend.

So that it seems to me that in the general composition of a piece which has to do with her coming to terms with a grown-up world, and the values of a grown-up world, that her hopes for a sexual and marital union with this young man, this twenty-fourth, if you will recall—the first nineteen didn't count, but the others began to count because she began to look for some satisfaction for herself as well as the boy in her relationship—this was the one she pinned her hopes on. And when this was dashed, her bitterness burst its bonds and she went berserk.

Q. Doctor, in your opinion, would any portion of this film be offensive to the American public?

A. Of course. Of course it would be offensive. I think for the wrong reasons, but—

THE COURT: I don't think you asked him the reasons; did you?

Q. Well, would you care to comment or to elaborate on your statement, Doctor?

A. I would assume that this Court doesn't need to be told about the double standard about sex in these United States. There has always been one standard of conduct and another standard [of] what we do or talk about. This film enters right into the heart of the matter, if I might say so, in one of the most taboo areas we as Americans have.

I scrounged about in the last few days looking for data about what we know about mouth-genital contact and I could find nothing more recent, that I found reliable, than the Kinsey reports of 1948 for men and 1953 for women. . . . The Kinsey data indicates that well over 60 percent of their sample of Americans have mouth-genital contact.

THE COURT: I am sorry, I didn't hear you. Have—

THE WITNESS: Over 60 percent have mouth-genital contact, your Honor.

Q. Doctor, from your professional point of view, is the attitude toward sex as depicted in the film a healthy one?

A. Yes. I would say it even stronger. It seems to me that sex is used in this film by the director, or the writer, to represent the close, warm, tender, human, body-to-body contact of two people who care about one another. . . .

Mr. Schilling cross-examined Dr. Hornick.

Q. Is it your testimony, Doctor, that a majority of Americans have intercourse in trees?

A. I don't have any data on that.

THE COURT: Does Kinsey?

A. Kinsey didn't study that variable.

THE COURT: The answer is no, Kinsey has no data on that?

THE WITNESS: Yes.

Q. Would your answer be the same for the balustrade of a public building with a sentry watching?

A. I didn't study the Kinsey data with that point in mind, but to the best of my memory from reading both volumes there is no data on balustrade sex. . . .

Q. In the absence of your recollection of any mention of this subject in the Kinsey report, is it your testimony, Doctor, that you are unable to tell us whether 60 percent of Americans have had intercourse in trees, or whether 60 percent of Americans have had intercourse on the balustrades of public buildings?

A. If you will recall, I think I was precise in saying that the Kinsey data validates that 60 percent of Americans have had mouth-genital relationships in their adult life. I made no qualification about balustrades or trees.

Q. You said that this film would be offensive to most Americans; is that correct?

A. I think it might offend many Americans. I have no data, but I know that mouth-genital contact, masturbation, and nudity raise hackles.

Q. When you say "might," would it? Is that the best you can do on the question based on your knowledge as a psychiatrist, the treatment of patients, and so forth? Is that as definite as you can be, that it might offend?

A. I said very definitely that I thought it would offend because of the long-standing prejudice of Americans about discussing, looking at, or confronting their own sexual behavior. . . .

But you know the higher the education of the person the more likely it is that the person himself or herself indulges in just that behavior. . . .

Dr. Thomas Levin, psychiatrist and associate professor of psychiatry at the Albert Einstein College of Medicine, examined by Mr. De Grazia, suggested that the film was religious.

Q. Would you define "religion" for the jury—that is, give your definition of it before you go on.

A. Yes. The film is a cinematographic attempt to create a ritualistic presentation of fundamental moral and ethical questions which man must deal with in order to—how can I say—referee between his impulses and his commitment to other men and his society. In that sense it is a religious film. And the ritual is a way we standardize and repeat the lessons that we are concerned with. . . . The film has to do with timelessness and the lack of personal boundaries in the quest for identity within an ethical life, personally and socially. The film uses a device of a particular young woman's search for her identity as an individual in an interpsychic sense—that is, internally, in herself—as well as her search for identity in a larger world and with other people in a larger world.

In that search she has to grapple with two fundamental issues. Those issues are the amount of commitment, personal commitment, involvement—love, if you wish—that she has in her relationships with other people; and, secondly, the amount of responsibility that she has in her relationship to a larger society.

The film uses the political area for exploring her commitment to the larger society, and that issue comes around non-violence and peace. It uses on the personal level the shorthand of the expression of personal interpsychic organization, which is the sexual act, the sexual responses, and the sexual relatedness.

In both of these areas the young woman seeks through ritual—and I must emphasize this, that this is what struck me most about this, that this is a series of rituals—she seeks through ritual to establish a fundamental truth: Who she is in relationship to other people, people close to her, and her society.

That would be my estimate of the basic themes.

Q. When you speak of rituals in the film, Doctor, would you give some examples of that?

A. Certainly. In the political or social area you have the young lady going through a series of interviews, and the cinematographic artist chooses to present these interviews as little slices in which there is a questioning and a response. That questioning and response is repetitive. Sometimes the same person appears at different points responding the exact same way. The responses tend to be —I don't mean this as a literary judgment, but rather an emotional judgment—somewhat boring. And that is an attempt to create through repetition that which is common, that which is frequent, that which is unexciting. . . .

That ritual, that kind of thing, is what the nature of a ritual was, a repetition over and over again in order to elicit a fundamental common response.

It reminds me very much of responsive readings in houses of worship.

The second area of ritual is in the sexual area. I was very struck, and amused almost, that the sexual content of the film enters quite late in the film, actually, and its entrance into the life of the film takes place in rather, I thought, amusing circumstances: The young man and the young lady involved have a great deal of difficulty dealing with realities, like I think getting a mattress in place, clearing off a hassock and books. . . .

There are many, many items which can be noted as ritual, including the clear presentation of the woman's search for ritual in her flirtation with Buddhism and meditation.

Again one of the most striking things is the ending note of the film, which I might note I felt was excessively moralistic in that the film, seems to say in the ending note that the wages of sin are disease. And then there is a scene which is a washing in the blood of the lamb, if I may use that expression, the baptism recreated, and they are washed from head to foot ritualistically in two side by side establishments in which they are attempted to be cleaned of the itch, I think it is referred to, but actually is a ritual to cleanse the soul.

The film then follows their interpersonal relationships in that the real sin is that they are both dishonest, and the young man some place—and I only saw the film once—in this area around this period expunges himself of his basic dishonesty, which is his dishonest relationship with a mistress, and discusses how he must end this, and also discusses his responsibility for his child, while the young woman involved makes her act of contrition and honesty by directly confronting the director, who in a sense is a certain kind of patron, and indicating that she is forfeiting a dishonest relationship, and then they both leave together.

Q. Are you suggesting, Doctor, that this film indicated some growth in the characters, ethical growth?

A. Most definitely on the young woman's part. There is the overt evidence which seemed to be on the young man's part. As a clinician, I have some doubts—because he so clearly is portrayed as a psychopath—he could be redeemed so easily; but the young woman: I was very touched, for instance, with her resolution of a basic human conflict which I thought was so kindly and so beautifully and so sensitively portrayed in the film, which is her relationship with her father. I thought that was most touching, since this is the developmental task of young people. It was done very beautifully in the film. . . .

Q. What scene are you referring to, Dr. Levin?

A. I am referring to the scene where, after a very stormy and critical relationship between daughter and father there is a rapprochement. They come together, this daughter and father who in my clinical judgment have been bound in a very frightening and impendingly disastrous Oedipal relationship, about their mutual troubles, and the daughter reaches toward the father for the first time with real warmth—which in the nature of the film one would suspect would be charged with a good bit of sexual energy—and the father, who has been portrayed as a weak character once frightened at the task of being a father with a seductive daughter, I thought he dealt with that beautifully by singing a little Swedish folk song, apparently, in which he says so very—talking about a river, and it ends by saying —but young women must have young men who can dance.

That made me well up with tears, I thought it was so beautifully done, very beautifully.

Q. In your opinion, does this film deal with the question of individual responsibility?

A. This film brings in a contemporary saint to discuss the issue of individual responsibility, and in the film we have the presentation of the saint, Martin Luther King, who is presented as a saint should be presented, as setting parameters.

And the young woman in her internal dialogue with Martin Luther King keeps asking the question of individual responsibility. I think most definitely her whole search is for a change from a young woman. A young woman is portrayed clearly at the beginning. The director's rejection of her is clear. He says, "You have no mind and no commitment." And she says, "Yes, but I go to bed with you and I act. What else do you want?"

And the director obviously wants more of a person than pure narcissism and self-interest. I am not quite sure I understand why this sets off the pursuit for greater meaning in her life, but that becomes the whole issue: what is her responsibility as an individual? . . .

I am not sure I responded to your question. Yes is the answer, if you ask if this is a search for great ethical commitment. And if it is attained. I think that is so. There is significant growth.

THE COURT: May I interrupt, Doctor? Would you state what you mean by ethical?

THE WITNESS: Yes, sir. Ethics, to a psychoanalyst at least—

THE COURT: No, to you.

THE WITNESS: Personally, sir?

THE COURT: What you mean by ethical. All I want to know is what you mean when you used that adjective.

THE WITNESS: Yes. I use ethics within the theoretical framework—

THE COURT: Couldn't you give me a short definition?

THE WITNESS: All right.

THE COURT: Isn't everything that man does ethical? Can it be defined rather briefly?

THE WITNESS: Ethics is to be distinguished from morality. Morality is a—

THE COURT: Don't tell me what morality is. My question is: Can you tell me what you mean by ethics?

THE WITNESS: Yes. Ethics are those parameters of behavior which are determined by an individual's scrutiny of his life, its purposes, and the integrity of his total personality.

THE COURT: That is an individual appraisal?

THE WITNESS: That's correct.

THE COURT: Thank you. . . .

Q. Dr. Levin, would you mind characterizing briefly for the jury the sexual attitude of Lena? Was she trying to do something in this area? Did she succeed in doing it? Did she resolve any important problems for herself?

A. Lena's sexual activity in the film in itself is not particularly noteworthy. What is most remarkable about the film is the attempt to integrate her sexual activity as part of her total personality. And so while her total personal search is to attain warmth and closeness, reconciliation, acceptance, as seen with her father, for instance, in her sexual attitudes it is as though the film shows a freedom of the form of sexual activity without a knowledge of the content of the emotional relationship which I think changes in the film as she gains awareness of the difference between sterile, formal sexuality and experimentation and truly spontaneous expression of sexuality which reflects the mood and temper of the relationship. . . .

Dr. Levin was cross-examined by Mr. Schilling.

Q. I believe you said that the sexual activity in the film is not particularly noteworthy. Would you explain the reasons for that statement?

A. . . . The activity itself is not noteworthy. I want to clarify that. It is not noteworthy in that it seems to deal with largely what young people deal with. Young people are involved in experimentation in position and place. In my clinical practice—and I am not prepared to become a sociologist on that—and in my discussions with young people, I have run across many a situation where sexual activity has taken place in unusual places with great thrill, and that may be the park or the chemistry laboratory in a college, or things of this sort. So that the experimentation in position and place is fairly commonplace. Young people are supposed to do that, I presume.

The other elements are the sexual acts—fellatio, cunnilingus. I did pick up the end of Dr. Hornick's testimony. I can't give you national statistics; I can tell you that they are very common activities. And in clinical practice—I just haven't seen in my entire clinical practice, except for children, a single adult who has not either indulged in fellatio or cunnilingus, or wished to or grappled with their concern about wanting to and being ashamed about it or being revulsed by it, and knowing that they really want to. It is very common.

Q. Was your statement that the sexual activity was not particularly noteworthy—were you making that statement in terms of the significance of the sexual activity in the film, the meaning that it had for the film?

A. No, no. I said that the activity itself was not noteworthy. I think it is to the director's credit that he attempted to do something that analysts have been trying to do for years, which is to talk about what is the language of communication involved in sexual activity. Because sexual activity is not just sexual, it is a communications attempt. And the film attempts to portray that communication.

Q. What I am trying to learn, Doctor, is whether you think the sexual scenes are noteworthy and are significant, and if you do think they have significance I would like to ask you what that significance is.

MR. DE GRAZIA: I think he has answered that several times.

THE COURT: Once more will nail it down then.

Q. . . . For example, the intercourse on the balustrade

in view of the sentry, what is the significance of that scene?

A. It is: make love not war. It is a social statement: make love not war.

Q. Anything else?

A. It is mildly exhibitionistic in a protected circumstance. It shows good ego function because if one has to be an exhibitionist one should choose an audience that cannot respond overtly. Other than that, nothing. . . .

Q. What significance in your view of the film was there to the scene of intercourse in the tree?

A. I think it was very amusing. I think it was a small touch of the absurd in that I think all man tries in his small and individual personal activity to reach a greater parameter. I think the two young people who say "we are having intercourse in the largest tree in Europe," as an effort of obtaining special significance, is humorous; it is a kind of touch of the absurd. . . .

Mr. Irving Fishman, Commissioner of Customs in New York, the government bureau responsible for seizing I Am Curious—Yellow, *was examined by Mr. De Grazia.*

Q. Did you order the seizure of the film *I Am Curious—Yellow*?

A. I did.

Q. How many times did you see this film before you decided to seize it?

A. Once.

Q. How many other employees of the Customs Bureau saw the film before your decision to seize it?

A. At the New York Customs Office, one other employee. . . .

Q. Have you ever worked for any educational, cultural or scientific organization, Mr. Fishman?

A. Do I belong to any?

Q. Have you ever worked for any?

A. No. I have spent my entire working career in the Bureau of Customs.

Q. Would you please briefly state your educational background.

A. I believe you asked me about my educational background; is that it?

Q. Yes.

A. I attended the College of the City of New York. I studied business administration. I obtained my degree in that subject. I attended the public schools in New York City. . . .

Q. Would you please state whether the film *I Am Curious—Yellow* in your opinion presents ideas or themes having social, political, religious, or other value. . . .

A. Social value. As I understand it— . . . as I understand social value it relates to the advocacy of ideas. These ideas may relate to art, science, drama, poetry—in fact, dance and sex.

Q. At the time that you were considering whether *I Am Curious* should be detained by your office at Customs, did anyone call to your attention the existence of a considerable number of reviews concerning the film appearing in Swedish and other foreign newspapers? . . .

A. When I saw these reviews I had already made up my mind to seize the film. The physical action, the preparation of the documents, perhaps, was not completed, but my decision had been made when I saw the reviews.

Q. Could you have changed your decision if you had read these reviews and been persuaded that the reviews required you to give another decision?

A. No, I don't think so.

Q. You couldn't have changed your decision?

A. No. . . .

On cross-examination by Mr. Schilling:

. . . We see— We pass on the average of a thousand

films a year, imported foreign films. I have never, in my forty years of experience, had presented to us in Customs a motion-picture film obviously intended for entertainment purposes that consisted of hard-core pornography. And so my decision was immediate in this case.

MR. GALLEN: Objection.

THE COURT: Much too late.

MR. GALLEN: It is not too late to be stricken from the record, your Honor.

THE COURT: But nobody so moved.

MR. GALLEN: I move right now that it be stricken from the record.

THE COURT: Yes. I will grant it. . . .

MR. SCHILLING: Mr. Fishman, I believe you testified that in the past two years you have personally seen about twenty-five American feature films; is that correct?

A. That's correct.

Q. Have you, in the course of these two years, acquired information about American feature films in ways other than actually seeing the film?

A. Well, we subscribe to the motion-picture trade papers. We read the reviews published in these papers. We see a great deal of motion-picture film in connection with our work, and naturally I try as much as possible in my personal life to see those films which have aroused curiosity and discussion in newspapers, plus, of course, motion-picture films which are not controversial at all.

I seek entertainment, and I try to keep away from the controversial films, except in connection with my duty. . . .

Q. Mr. Fishman, would you state the opinion you formed with respect to *I Am Curious* when you viewed it prior to your decision to seize it? . . .

A. I felt that the dominant theme of the film was sex. The scene of sex intercourse on the floor of Lena's room, the scene of intercourse on the balustrade, the one in the tree, the one in the lake, the scene in the cottage—

several scenes of fornication in the cottage, the scenes of fellatio, the scenes of cunnilingus—these helped me make up my mind rather quickly. . . .

Q. Would you tell us more fully what your opinion was with regard to the value of this film in connection with your decision to seize the film?

A. I explained in my earlier testimony that social value may advance ideas concerning sex. I admit that interspersed through the film there were some other ideas expounded.

I saw the film four times totally, but I did not leave the projection room with any message, no thought.

There were many scenes, interviews between Lena and the public officials of the Swedish government, but they conveyed no real social import to me. . . .

Q. Have you read *Memoirs of a Woman of Pleasure* by Joseph Cleland?

A. I didn't get that at all.

THE COURT: Have you read *Memoirs?*

Q. (*continuing*) Have you read *Fanny Hill?*

A. Many times.

Q. Is that a book which in your judgment is almost exclusively dealing with sex and sexual relations?

A. Yes.

Q. Is that a book which in your judgment nevertheless may have redeeming social importance?

A. My own view—

THE COURT: He is asking for your own opinion, yes.

A. (*continuing*) No. . . .

Q. Do you know that the Supreme Court of the United States has in effect ruled that that book has redeeming social importance?

A. Yes. . . .

Q. In reaching your judgment concerning the question of redeeming social importance in the film *I Am Curious—Yellow,* is it your testimony that you balanced or weighed the social values or ideas of social value expressed in the film against the sexual material?

A. I gave all of the constitutional protection, the tests which we have to apply before we make a decision, consideration. The Bureau of Customs is not the final word in the determination as to whether material is obscene. Our function is merely to seek out that which we believe should be referred to the Court for final decision.

Your questions are directed to me as though I make the final decision. The Courts have told us that we are not to conjecture and study and spend a great deal of time weighing one phase of the matter against the other.

I believe that this film was sufficiently objectionable so that it should be referred to the Court for a final determination as to whether it is obscene.

Q. Mr. Fishman, I don't think you quite answered my question. I am trying to find out whether or not you weigh the social values that you find in a work against what you consider its prurient appeal in reaching your judgment of whether or not to seize.

A. Yes.

Q. You do weigh that?

A. Yes.

Q. It is also your testimony that you try to follow as best you can the decisions of the Federal Courts of this country with regard to obscenity?

A. Yes.

Q. Are you familiar with the case of *Jacobellis* vs. *Ohio* in the Supreme Court of the United States, decided in 1964, concerning motion-picture film?

THE COURT: I am not going to permit you to ask this man any of those questions, whether he applied the right tests or the wrong tests or applied them wrongly or inadvertently. That is not our problem here today.

Mr. Ned Polsky, associate professor of sociology at the State University of New York at Stony Brook, was examined by Mr. De Grazia.

Q. Are there ideas of any importance to you as a sociologist presented in this film, that is, ideas of social importance?

A. Yes. A good many. One, for example, would be the question of the extent to which it is possible to change a society. Lena, I think, goes through a good deal of questioning herself and others about this: To what extent political action can be really effective? Do we have to put up with things as they are, or should we try to change them? Other questions: the nature of politics, whether or not it is possible to adhere to a code of complete non-violence; the theme of violence versus non-violence as an ethical problem and as a psychological problem is portrayed very thoroughly in the film, both in relation to politics and to sex or sexual relations.

Q. Why are these ideas or themes important to you?

A. They are basic questions about— Well, essentially, let me put it this way: Sociology is the study of the nature of society and what is true of people by virtue of the fact that they live in a society; and the film, I think, explores a lot of these questions: the question of whether we can, for instance, adhere to a code of complete non-violence, no matter how frustrated, how angry we feel, and so on. And to me the most moving individual scene in the film, actually, is where Lena breaks down and says to Martin Luther King, "I can't make it. I can't really stick to that non-violent bit"—you know, something like that, some words to that effect. To me it was a very moving part of her struggle.

Q. Did this film present an answer in terms of the problems you have just discussed?

A. Yes and no. The film, I don't think, leaves one—or

at least didn't leave me—with any easy answers. But I think it presented, and I think it would present, especially to young people, the answer that it is necessary to struggle, it is necessary to try to find out the answers for yourself to these questions, not take any of these questions about politics or sex or the nature of society and so on, not take any of these questions for granted, that it is important to try to find out.

I think that would be the main, ultimate message, if you like, of the film. I think especially for young people that would be a message that the film would convey.

Q. Is there any social importance in the relationship with her father, with the heroine's father and with the older generation?

A. Yes. I would say that the relation with the father is one aspect of a theme that runs through the film in other scenes as well; for instance, in her interviews with Swedish tourists who have just come back from a visit to Spain, or in her interviews with labor officials—the theme of the younger generation often feeling that the older generation has made its peace with society, that it has in a way given up the struggle to change the society, has gotten too secure in its occupational positions to risk basic questioning of the society and so on, a theme which is one aspect of this, you know, struggle between the generations that is going on in the United States, of course, today, not just Sweden.

Q. Would you explain that, the relationship to the United States?

A. Well, I think we see it all around us. There is hardly a day goes by where one doesn't see in the newspaper young people protesting this or that aspect of the way the older generation is running things, sometimes getting quite violent about it, too, as in the case of, let's say, what has been going on up at Columbia University recently.

And you see also the theme, too, the question of violence against non-violence. . . .

Q. Is this aspect of uncovering of, in your judgment, facts which exist but which are not usually portrayed of sociological importance?

A. Certainly. Sociology is concerned basically with trying to portray the society as it is, whether we like it or not. Some of the things we find out we are very unhappy about. We would rather they were not true, you know.

We are concerned to find out, you know, what in fact is the case regarding sex or politics or anything else, whether it makes us happy or unhappy.

This is the point of any kind of scientific investigation.

And I think the film is quite valuable in doing just that, in portraying sex, first of all, as being bound up with all sorts of other things, not as a separate area of one's life but as being related to how one feels about politics, how one feels about one's parents, how one feels about the nature of the society one is in. The film, I think, is very realistic in portraying how all of these things are related to one another. I think if any one of them were cut out, as it were, it would damage the significance of the film and damage its power to move people. . . .

Q. You testified earlier that you have made sociological studies of pornography. Does that include pornographic films?

A. Yes.

Q. Could you tell the jury what in your opinion are the features of pornographic films? . . .

A. Yes. These films have several things in common. One of them is that the predominant material in the film is sex. The other elements of plot or character are either totally absent or just a scaffolding. That is, most of the film, most of the time, most of the actual running minutes of the film has to do with sex as a graphic—

Q. When you say "most" do you mean seventy-five percent, ninety percent, fifty percent?

A. Well, certainly well over three quarters of the running time, say, deals with actual portrayals of sexual acts and/or nudity. That would be one feature common to all of these films.

Another is that sex is treated in a fantasy way. There are no problems. There is no need for contraception. There are no unwanted pregnancies. There are no irreconcilable conflicts between the sexual partners. It is a kind of never-never land, in which both the man and the woman are eternally lustful and energetic and insatiable and so on, a kind of fantasy way of treating sex.

What else? Those, I would say, would be the two main distinguishing features of all of these pornographic films.

Q. In your judgment, in your opinion, are either of these elements of pornography present in the film *I Am Curious—Yellow*?

A. Not at all. Quite the contrary. Not only do the actual sexual portrayals take up a minority of the running time of the film, at least as I remember it, but even in those sexual episodes they are often portrayed in such a way that they don't function the way the sex in these pornographic films does.

For instance, in this film *I Am Curious*, unlike any pornographic film I have ever seen, you never see the man with an erection. You never see actual penetration of the man into the vagina of the woman. These are two staples of any and every pornographic film.

Secondly, the sex often takes place in settings where it is difficult to be sexually aroused, because the text is treated satirically. They are doing it on this balustrade, sort of as a gesture of contempt for the King and the soldiers and so on.

In other words, the sex is placed in a context in which

it would be very difficult for the audience to be sexually aroused.

Again, this is very unlike pornographic films....

On cross-examination by Mr. Schilling:

Q. Let us consider the scene of intercourse in the pond or the lake. How would the film lose in social value if that scene were not in the picture?

A. That scene is part of the theme of violence and non-violence, and there, one of the messages to me in that scene is that often violent behavior, violent quarrels, are seemingly resolved—that is to say, people attempt to resolve them by engaging in sexual intercourse.

You remember what immediately precedes this intercourse or apparent intercourse—we never actually see it—but apparent intercourse in this pond, is some kind of violent quarrel, in which the girl takes, I think, his gloves and throws them out in the water, and they have some argument, and she goes and gets them, and then he goes out and grabs her, and there is some kind of struggle, which looks at first very violent, as if he may even be going to drown her, and then it immediately turns into a sexual kind of thing.

And I think that is a very realistic kind of portrayal of the psychology of human beings.

The Reverend Dan M. Potter, Executive Director of the Protestant Council, City of New York, and chairman of that organization's Committee on Motion Pictures, was called as the Government's only witness; Mr. Schilling examined him.

Q. Do you recall the scene of intercourse in the film on the balustrade of a public building, with a sentry looking on?

A. Yes; I do recall.

Q. From a religious viewpoint, in your opinion can it be said with any validity that the portrayal of sex in that scene is sanctified?

A. Is sanctified?

Q. Yes.

A. It is the most ridiculous thing I ever heard of. . . .

Q. . . . Do you recall the scene where the male lead takes the rifle away from the girl and throws her on the ground, lifts her dress up? Do you recall that scene?

A. Yes; I do.

Q. From the religious viewpoint, would there be any validity to the opinion that the sex portrayed in that scene is sanctified?

A. Well, no. I am wondering what the definition of sanctification is in this setting. Normally, "sanctified" implies that this is in a religious context, in which God is blessing a relation, and usually the marriage service; in most all of our communions is a marriage service in which a prayer of invocation, asking God to sanctify this union or to bless this union, is what we normally think of as sanctification.

I can't imagine throwing a girl down, out on a street someplace, or, as in this instance, in front of a building, and virtually equivalent to raping her, being considered sanctified. It certainly would have no theological justification in the way that word is usually used in theological terms.

Q. Is there any theological justification for the following definition of "sanctified"? "Sanctified in the sense that it was a part of the creation believed by the Creator and given as part and parcel of the human condition and the human situation for the enjoyment and perpetuation of the human species"?

A. Well, a portion of that would be orthodox, would be in the same sense that I was using it before, in a setting of a formal service where prayers are involved and God is asked to bless a relation. In that sense the word "sanctification" is used.

As I gather from the way you have read the statement there, that the author of the statement is saying that any relation that appears to be natural is sanctified by the Creator or by God. I think that is not applicable to this situation. This is not a natural relation, and it certainly is not believed by God in the way that this is being conducted, by any orthodox interpretation of theology that I know of. . . .

Mr. Gallen cross-examined Dr. Potter.

Q. Dr. Potter, have you ever testified before in court in a proceeding brought by the Customs Office to seize and destroy a film?

A. Yes; I have.

Q. Would you please tell the jury the case in which you so testified?

A. I testified in *491* and in *Erotikon.*

Q. For whom did you testify?

A. For the Government.

Q. And would you tell the jury the result in both cases?

A. I don't know.

MR. SCHILLING: Objection, your Honor.

THE COURT: Wait—

MR. GALLEN: No further questions.

The director of I Am Curious—Yellow, *Mr. Vilgot Sjöman, came to the United States from his native Sweden to testify on behalf of his film.*

Q. Would you state the names of the five films which you have directed?

A. The first one was called *The Mistress.* The second *491.* The third was called *The Dress.* The fourth was called *My Sister, My Love.* And this one.

Q. The fifth is *I Am Curious—Yellow*?

A. Yes. And the sixth one being *I Am Curious—Blue*.

Q. *I Am Curious—Blue* is a different film from *I Am Curious—Yellow*?

A. Yes.

Q. Would you explain the difference, please, briefly?

A. They are made in the same way and the same style and the same stories are repeated again. I would say, to make it short, that it also starts from the same beginning and ends in the same way, but in the *Yellow* and in the *Blue* you get a different side of Swedish life in each.

Q. Would you tell the jury, please, the significance of blue and yellow?

A. This is the national colors of Sweden, yellow and blue, and I wanted to tell that this is the same film, but I also wanted to separate them, and the best way to do it was to put the colors on them, I thought. . . .

Q. What was the dominant theme of this film?

A. I wanted to make a portrait of Sweden right now in the late '60s as I experienced my country. I started out by thinking of it as a kaleidoscope, because I didn't want to limit my ideas to a narrow and written screenplay, but I wanted to have a large form in which all kinds of ideas could be used, ideas that somehow reflected the conflicts and the climate of Sweden right now. That is to say, that a lot of the things in the film are referring to what is actually going on and bringing the discussion and some of the questions in Swedish political and social life onto the screen, which hasn't been done before in our country.

Q. What are some of those social and political themes?

A. One thing that is illustrated in the film is the question of [a] republic or abolishing [the] monarchy. There are several references to that. And that is part of the main theme, that I wanted to discuss and portray the feeling you have about the Social Democratic government that has been in power for thirty years, and the question if they have succeeded in approaching a classless society or not, what kind of hopes for the future, and what feelings of failure you do have. So there are several examples of that kind.

Q. Would you give a few examples of how you explored that then?

A. Yes. The labor movement is very well organized and established, and the system is [that] every two years, every year, is brought up the question of the payment of the laborers. And you have a feeling of a great distance somehow between the actual working people and the labor movement. And so we entered the labor unions, their headquarters, and asking them questions in a simple way how they felt about the class structure of the Swedish society. That is one thing.

We approached [a] minister in the government, Mr. Palme, and asked him what he thought about the present state concerning the classless society. And then we asked people in reference to—there is a big trend, all Swedes are traveling to Spain, for the moment to Mallorca and the Canary Islands, and it is surprising to me that they don't have any—that it doesn't present any problems, apparently, to them—or does it? We ask all this kind of question. And then we went out to ask them in interviews.

And then the question of how Swedish young people do react to what is going on in the world of today, the relation between dissatisfaction at home and concern for the rest of the world, reflected in the demonstrations which are actually taken from actual things going on.

Q. Would you try to explain the ways in which you developed some of the other moral and social problems which in your judgment are confronting Swedish youth today? . . .

A. I will put it this way. If you are going to make a portrait of your own country, what is going on, you are making documentaries, interviewing people. Then if you don't have a focus for that theme, somebody who is trying to understand this won't get any feeling for it. So that was the main reason for building the film around Lena, the theme being that you must be concerned with this little girl who is a simple, ordinary kind of girl with a lot of ideas and feelings, and you will feel how she is developing, how she is reacting toward her society.

So that is why I by and by developed things around her, and the main theme being the relation to the father and disappointment in the father, and then her relation to the boys, then mainly one boy. And, of course, I think in portraying Lena we tried to portray a very sort of new and modern kind of girl that hasn't been portrayed very much on the screen, a girl who asks for the same freedom as men always have done, and who is sort of unconscious of what is going on inside her.

She has a lot of emotion that she doesn't know about. She tries to behave with the same freedom as the boy, and the same attitudes. The whole thing being her story while she discovered that inside herself is going on things she didn't know about and doesn't know how to handle.

But I am thinking of her as a portrait of a new kind of female, young female, coming in the front light of our country. . . .

Q. Did you also in making this film, Mr. Sjöman, seek to make, to explore new techniques in film making, techniques which are new for you, or perhaps otherwise, in the film world?

A. Yes; I surely did.

Q. Would you mind describing a little bit what you did, to the jury? What you tried to do?

A. Well, from my point of view, it was sort of liberation from the school I had been going to when I went to Bergman's school and was a pupil of him—and he was building very strict scripts, which you had to stick to, and then you had the whole equipment of the studio, and you had all kinds of traditions and ideas in film making.

And then I said I better break with this and go out on my own and invent things, and especially I felt that I could, if I came close to the actor[s] and could discuss with them very openly about certain things that came along, I could get their experience. . . .

I got in touch with young actors and said, "Look: What is your experience? How do you experience life, and what should you do in this situation?"

I didn't force my ideas upon them. I tried not to. A lot of the material and the attitudes in the film is brought in by the help of the actors. I have an idea about what a young girl is, and Lena had another idea about what a young girl is, and these two ideas clashed or merged, and I felt that I got more close to realities with the help of the actors. It is such a technical thing to describe how you work with the material. I can say that, in short, it was a sort of experimental field, where I tried different techniques, bringing myself and the crew into the film, playing, so to speak, with reality. I mean, the audience would suspect that the main situation between Lena and me was the real one. Of course, Lena and I knew perfectly what was the reality, but we played with this impression that this is the full reality we are presenting on the screen.

You can say that I moved in the difficult field of psychodrama, where you try to take the experience of yourself or the actors, use that in the film, in the making of a play or a film. . . .

Q. How do you feel now about the film?

A. Well, then if I try to look objectively on what I have been doing, I can say I think I succeeded in two things: One was bringing the political discussion of my country into the movies, which hadn't been done before, and people had asked for that. They didn't feel that movies were close to their life. And I think I actually succeeded in bringing that to the screen.

And also I think that in the ways of portraying Lena and Börje's love story, I think I accomplished something which was good, because I succeeded to a certain extent in breaking away from a lot of artistic clichés about how love scenes should be made.

Mr. Sjöman was cross-examined by Mr. Schilling.

Q. Mr. Sjöman, would you elaborate on the statement that you succeeded in this picture in breaking away from artistic clichés in making scenes of love-making?

A. Yes. I have been making four films, and every time the actors and I have to cope in these films with the love situation where love and sex are going to be portrayed, I felt that we were very traditional, and we relied upon clichés of American, French, and Swedish films, a very heavy tradition of clichés, and I felt stuck with it and said, "This is not fresh; it is not the way people behave. I am not achieving something as an artist if I am just sticking to these clichés."...

And so in most cases I asked Lena and Börje, "How do you feel about this, as young people? How would you approach this girl? How do you think she behaves in this case"—and so forth and so on. So they came up with their ideas about it, confronting my ideas.

And I think I have succeeded to some extent of breaking down—of getting away from the clichés. What I feel is missing is, of course, is a more mature relationship, the warmth and the tenderness that you have in a more mature relationship. This is a very young love story. You have two people who are sort of using each other's bodies. It gives a sort of chilly atmosphere around it.

After making the film, I said if I could make the love scene something like this, and I could have the same warmth and the same human atmosphere as I feel I have succeeded in one scene of the film, that is, the one scene between the girl and her father in the shop—he is drinking wine and singing, and the girl goes—is going—through all kinds of emotional stages—that scene, to my mind, with the help of the actors, has become very warm. It has all the humanity.

And I think if I succeeded in merging this—to doing non-conventional, not cliché sex scenes, with all the warmth of that scene, then I should achieve something the next time.

Q. In your answer you made no mention of any personal inhibitions that entered into this situation. Is it not correct that one of the reasons for desiring to break these sexual clichés is that you yourself felt personally inhibited in your work as a director in making these love scenes?

MR. DE GRAZIA: I think he just answered that, your Honor.

THE COURT: Then we will have it once more.

A. Yes. I think I mentioned it when I said that every time in the first four films I had to make a love scene, I felt very inhibited, together with the actors, inhibited in the sense that instead of the good thing for a director or an artist in general to approach it fresh and say, "What is your experience? How do you feel about this? What does reality look like? How are you going to transpose that into your novel and your play and your film?"—instead of doing that, then you rely upon what is done everywhere else, and then you are bound to [come] away with a bad result.

So when you feel inhibited as a person, then you are sticking to the clichés. And I did that in those films.

Q. One of the things you were inhibited about was the portrayal of male nudity in films; is that not correct?

A. Not correct. I was inhibited in many ways. So I would say that this was my general problem as a director. I didn't know how to cope with sex or politics. . . .

I would like to say this: My experience during the making of the film was that at the beginning you think of portraying actual behavior with the help of the actors as very difficult . . . and then when we got together and discussed the things, we found that it didn't present so many problems of inhibitions as we thought.

You are asking for a self-analysis, which I am not really able to elaborate on too much, since I don't know myself that much. . . .

Q. You set out, did you not, to break sexual taboos in film making when you made *I Am Curious*?

A. I set out to break away from certain clichés of how love scenes should be made, yes. That I did.

Q. You set out to break sexual taboos, did you not?

A. I set out to break away from clichés in film making, yes. And if you do affect the sex taboos, then that is another thing that concerns society in general.

I was concerned with making the movie in the way I wanted to do it.

I don't understand your question. The reason why this becomes a little unclear to me, when you ask this question, you put such an emphasis on male nudity, so in my turn I would like to ask you why. There are certainly female nudity clichés, and the female body is exposed and used in all films that way, that is very familiar with everyone and everybody. So if you discuss nudity, I would like you to bring both up to discussion. . . .

I don't know if you have noticed that I tried not to do what is usually done in the films in point of view of sex, portraying the moment of orgasm. That is usually, very often, tried by symbols. I am not doing that in any place. I think the interesting thing is what is going on before and afterward, and I try to show that in these films.

Nothing is really happening in the mattress scene. They are just having a lot of trouble with the mattress and the clothes.

I would add one thing, too, which I think is important. People are so used in films to add things and read into the pictures things that are not there, especially American films. They work on two levels. They show one thing and then they expect the audience to fill in the gaps. You have a dissolve. They are kissing or embracing, and then you have a dissolve.

There are also all kinds of other ways to do this kind of trick. But the thing, the main thing, being that the movie audience is so used to read things into it, so when they are confronted with several of the realistic pictures in this film they continue to read things into it.

For instance, in the scene in the tree in the countryside what is actually presented is Lena and Börje trying out, with their clothes on, an undiscovered, a sort of funny sex position in the tree, but they have their clothes on. And then Börje starts to take off his pants, and then he approaches Lena, and then suddenly, as in real life, they are in the middle of discussing something else then, instead of having an intercourse—they are discussing her feelings for her body, and she has a confession, a sort of very tender confession to him, that she doesn't like her own body, and her first nineteen lovers didn't give her any pleasure.

This is often referred to as a sexual intercourse scene. I can only explain that in terms that the audience is so used to read into the pictures things that are not there. . . .

Q. Would you say it was generally correct that it was your objective in making this film with respect to the sex scenes to show things as they actually happened?

A. Yes, to break away from the ordinary way of presenting very arranged love scenes, and to approach reality and reconstruct reality, and to give the audience the feeling that this is more likely to be the real behavior than what is shown in many other films. But I must add one thing: that part of the intention is also to satirize, so there is also a lot of parody. Since you are particularly talking about the sex scenes now, there is a lot of parody and satire in the tree, in the pond, or the swamp, the balcony scene. All these are not supposed to be ordinary, realistic behavior but I am making fun of certain things.

Q. In the scene where Lena was fondling Börje's genitals, this is the scene in the country after the rifle is taken away from her, in the filming of that scene did Lena actually kiss Börje's penis?

A. If you mean—it is a question of touching. Do you mean if her lips actually touched his penis?

Q. Yes.

A. I can't answer that because I wasn't that close, and I can't tell from the image, either. I have a feeling it was possible for her just to have her lips a couple of millimeters above the penis. If she actually touched it or not I didn't ask her, or I didn't ask him, either. My experience with actors is that they sometimes enjoy the situation and they kiss very heavily in order to get emotional life out of it, and some of them—I am talking about ordinary kisses, mouth to mouth—and some of them are sort of chilly and just doing it technically, or sometimes touching beside the mouth. . . .

Mr. Norman Mailer was questioned by Mr. De Grazia.

Q. Are protest movements of the type you have written about the type also involved in the film *I Am Curious—Yellow*?

A. I felt there were great similarities. In looking at the film, one of the things in the film which fascinated me was the similarities and the differences between protest movements in Sweden and in America. I was impressed on the one hand with the sophistication of the protest movements in Sweden. Primarily because it is a European country, they are used to strife and profound disagreements between the citizens of the country. I was impressed with the almost good-humored air with which opponents talked to one another.

For example, the girl was questioning the tourists either going to or returning from Spain. Many of them seemed amused by her when she questioned their moral right to go to Spain. For me it was a sort of light air of comedy in various sections of the interviews. There was a sense of almost kittenish or puckish amusement about the seriousness of the girl, this militancy of the girl, the dedication of the girl, and the relative sophistication or simpleness of the people answering her. . . .

Q. Was the heroine in the film *I Am Curious—Yellow* involved in any protest or quasi-revolutionary groups?

A. It was my impression that she was, yes. Not in any formal sense. In other words, it seemed to me she, like so many of the young today—you know, the young today—my impression is that they do not believe in formal alliance with political parties the way they had to during the depression or shortly after the war. And so, like many of these young kids, she was around the fringes of these movements but in fact the fringes by now seem to be almost more important and impressive than the core in their numbers.

She was interested in the Russian Communists and what they had to say as personified by Yevtushenko's visit. She demonstrated in front of the Russian embassy. At one point in the picture she attacked America.

Like so many of these young children all over Europe and America, she was in a state of great obsession and interest with public affairs, and that I thought was typical of many American youths today. I felt that she was representative of the youth today not only in Europe but also in America, I would say. I wouldn't say that she reminded me exactly of an American girl, but reminded me of young people all over the world.

Q. Would you please state whether you felt the film *I Am Curious—Yellow* had artistic importance.

A. Well, if I may, could I take my time to get to that point, because the problem was a large one for me before I went to see the picture, and if I might I would like to present a deep reservation I had about the picture before I saw it because I think the question is attached to the answer. In other words, my preliminary remarks are attached very much to the answer about the artistic merit or lack of it in the film. . . . I have thought a lot about the problem of sexuality in movies. I have been obsessed with the problem and concerned with the problem and devoted to the problem in one way or another for twenty years of writing novels.

After all, this is not a simple moral problem. There has been a great preponderance of, let's say—put it this way: there have been many victories that have been won by people who believe in greater liberty in the arts, and I have been one of those people. I have been engaged in many of these campaigns. My own books very often were considered, certain of them, in their way, as opening new possibilities for liberty to write about sexual matters. But I have always been concerned about it because I don't think it is an easy liberty or a liberty that can be necessarily pursued promiscuously. I think it is a dangerous liberty.

In movies, of course, this danger is more obvious and more self-evident because movies affect the emotions so powerfully. Before I saw this movie, therefore, I was a little bothered because I had a feeling for a long time that the history of movie-making was moving to the point implicit from the beginning, to the point where through stages the makers of serious movies and serious actors finally come to showing actors engage in sexual intercourse on the screen. Everything in its history shows that it is moving to that point, and this film comes closer than any picture we have yet seen.

So when I heard about it I had already written in *Esquire* about a year ago that I did not know if I as a film director even welcomed this; it bothered me very much. The reason it bothered me is something that has a deep relation to the problem of the actor in Western civilization.

The actor began as someone universally despised. The actor let's say five hundred years ago was despised because they felt that the actor was doing something that was half diabolical; he was playing with emotions, considered a dangerous thing to do. Women weren't allowed to be actresses in the beginning, in the Elizabethan theater.

This distrust and uneasiness carried to the modern time where, since we are vastly more liberal, progressive, and open-minded about these matters, we tend to accept the actor kissing the actress.

Actually, the problem remains—and it is a deep problem —because if the actor and the actress devote themselves to a sexual act in order to create art, then you get to the point where art then is becoming more important than the sexual act, and that is an enormously moral matter to me, because if art is getting more important than the sexual act, then we are involved in a debasement of the sexual act.

So I approached this movie with great trepidation because I felt that I might not like this movie, I might find that it would profoundly violate my sense of what is proper in these very dangerous matters, because I felt there was something very uneasy to me about the thought of an actor and actress becoming engaged in such acts that deeply for the sake of art.

When I saw the picture I was extraordinarily moved by it in a quiet way. I thought I would find the picture uninteresting from what I had heard about it ahead of time, the way it had been spoken of in various announcements, and from what I had heard of it from the contesting parties. I had the impression the picture would prove to be a shocker with a lot of dull matter. In other words, I had the impression it was going to be a documentary with a lot of overt sexual matter, and it would be interesting only because you have the problem posed of what you are going to do about it.

I was not prepared for a picture of the artistic dimension of this one. I think it is one of the finest and best pictures I have seen in a long time, and I was very moved by it, and I found that in fact I was somewhat overcome by it because I felt the portrayal of the girl in that is almost bewitching, because she is so complex.

I was left in a curious way when the picture was over. I was left with a sense of deep admiration, almost of awe, for the complex and mysterious nature of women. I thought that the particular forms of suffering and self-discovery she goes through in that picture, that odd mixture of coquetry and childlikeness in her, that sense of almost zaniness in her, opposed to the bitterness in her, and the cruelty in her, and the sense of someone partly beautiful, partly crippled emotionally, sort of very ordinary on the one hand, sort of magical on the other—I thought that a magnificent creation. I thought how mysterious we are as people.

So I thought while the picture moved into a terribly dangerous ground I could come on the stand and testify in its favor, to say I think it is a profoundly moral movie.

By that I don't mean it is a simple movie, or that the problems raised are absolutely answered by it. I think they are answered by it if we are willing to take the view that modern times are dangerous times and that we live in relation to a series of absurdities. So that, for example, we have thirty thousand people who are killed every year driving automobiles, which is more people than are killed in most wars, yet we don't say that we must dispense with the automobile because it is necessary to modern civilization.

So we have to deal dangerously in the arts with many of these matters. So I think this picture, while it deals in a dangerous fashion with dangerous subjects, nevertheless has a moral authority that left me with a feeling of awe. I felt I had encountered a major work.

I felt it was one of the most important motion pictures I have ever seen in my life because it attempts to deal with the nature of modern reality, the extraordinary complexity of modern reality.

There is the fact that on one hand we are witnesses to a documentary, so to speak, because as we are walking down the street someone interrogates us, asks our opinion about something. On the other hand, we are people with ideas, passionate people with ideas that we want to fulfill. Then we have personal complications in our life that do not necessarily have any relation to it. Sometimes they act exactly the opposite of our personal ideas as our contradictions reveal themselves. We are good and evil moment by moment. We are interesting, boring; we are tragic, comic. We are satiric. On top of that we don't know the nature of our reality because it keeps shifting.

I think ahead to a few years from now when we have home movie cameras and home video screens which seconds later reflect and mirror our actions, when we can start taking movies this second and can see them on the screen immediately. At that time we will have difficulty in distinguishing when does the reality begin, which is the reality, when you are being photographed, or five seconds later when you look at it on your own home individual screen?

In this picture there are a great many attempts to deal with the immensity of this problem. For instance, the director. You don't know whether these people are real actors or figures in a story; whether the director is a character in the picture or not. You see the cameramen in certain scenes and not in others. For instance, you see the cameramen being cameramen.

All these factors come together, I think, to produce a work of art which is a substantial and major work of art, and I think it is one of the more impressive movies I have seen in my life.

Q. Mr. Mailer, I think in part you began to answer my next question, but I would like you to state in your own way, if you can, any of the areas in which you felt this film had for you a moral or a social importance.

A. I think that I tried to cover that in what I had said earlier. I think the moral and social importance for me consisted of the fact that the director was in my mind a serious artist, in fact an artist with major talents, with large, powerful talents, who was attempting to perform the work of the artist, which is to present his vision of existence. The artist bears in the twentieth century an extraordinarily odd relation to society that he did not necessarily bear in other countries, because society is founded primarily upon law and the church, or, if you will, religion and law.

These have been the two main guidelines of society until the twentieth century. It is only in the twentieth century that we come to feel that despite the majesties of law, and of religion, that there is something accelerating in the twentieth century at such a fast rate that religion and law, by the very fact they are institutions, and stable institutions, are not changing quite so rapidly as the nature of life.

That does not mean religion and law are to be ignored or are valueless. It means people wander through more and more empty spaces not immediately touched upon by religion and law, and it is exactly in these empty spaces art comes in and attempts to deal with the nature of modern realities, the modern realities which make us make moral decisions every day of our lives.

Whenever we have to make a decision and have to decide is it good to do this or that or is it bad to do this or that, and we have no experience, we have no guideline, then we are in what people have come to call the modern condition; we are in a state of confusion. . . .

These spaces, as I would say, these empty moral spaces, these spaces where judgment is difficult because of the lack of experience or knowledge, are filled by artists well or badly. I think the importance of art in the twentieth century, the reason there is such enormous interest in the works of the artists, apart from the fact these works are now presented so quickly to the masses at large, is that artists by virtue of their freedom have the opportunity to attempt to give you their vision of society.

Modern society is so complex that very few artists ever can give you a vision that is of any use, and I found this vision of this director Sjöman to be extraordinary because it was comprehensive, because I could look at the life of these people in Sweden and have a feeling somehow or other, and I could hardly say why, that my own life now has a better sense of proportion. I began to see the absurdities, and the areas where these problems arose that I couldn't decide for myself, these terrible moral problems, began to have some focus.

The main thing about the picture was that it gave me a good feeling finally about men and women, particularly about this woman in this picture. I had a feeling they were all more noble than I thought before I saw the picture. The picture left me with a feeling of—I heard the word sanctity used here yesterday, and though I wouldn't use that word, I would say that I felt slightly shriven, a slightly more moral man, and that is a rare feeling to get from a movie.

The moral and social values are to me self-evidenced through the emotions that the picture aroused in me and left me with.

Q. Do you think the importance in these ways the film had for you and has for you can be shared by other persons in America, if they see the film?

A. Well, I can say that I think so. Of course, there is no further authority than the fact that I think so. To the extent that other people are like me, they will perhaps react in the same or similar fashion. I couldn't go further than that.

I think it is—I can only say I think it is a highly moral picture and at an extraordinarily sophisticated level of morality. It leaves us to deal with morality in an area where the most desperate chances have to be taken at times. In other words, someone who is profoundly religious could say that these actors may be endangering their mortal souls. Nevertheless, what we are given in return is an insight into the profoundly troubled and vital and tortured and magnificent and comic aspects of the sexual relation in young people who are living between ten ideologies and fifty different passions and ambitions.

Mr. Schilling cross-examined Mr. Mailer, first asking if he thought his own "opinion a reliable indication of whether the movie will or will not shock the American public?"

A. I will not pretend this movie is not going to shock anyone. Obviously, it will shock certain people. Any number of activities shock people. If a man walks down the street and he spits in the street, it will prove shocking to certain people.

Q. You said after you saw this movie you were left with a sense of awe about the mysterious nature of women?

A. Yes.

Q. You don't mean to suggest that before you saw the film you did not have a sense of awe about the mysterious nature of women?

A. No, you are absolutely correct. Before I saw the movie I had a sense of it; it was just that that sense was deepened by the movie.

Q. You stated that you were obsessed with the problem of sexuality in movies?

A. Yes. May I answer, or is your question not finished?

Q. My question to you is for you to state the ways in which you are obsessed with the problem of sexuality in movies.

A. Obsession is a particularly powerful word, and to me what it means—because it is a word on which there is not general agreement—is that you keep going back in your thoughts to this place and you don't have an answer. In other words, you keep going back to a point.

Let's say something happened in your life at a given moment that caused you some amount of difficulty, and you keep going back to that point and saying to yourself, was it my fault, was it her fault, could it have been avoided, was I evil, was I good? That sort of thing. We keep thinking about it and keep going back to it again and again.

For example, when we remember a friendship that has been broken up we keep trying to think, was it his fault, was it my fault? Such matters are obsessive.

When I say that in connection with movies what I mean by saying the idea of sexuality in movies is obsessive to me is that I have been concerned about this because I have seen it coming, I have seen the day coming when actors, by the logic of their art, would wish to indulge in sexual intercourse to fulfill the need of the picture.

I did not know how I felt about it. It was a burning matter. I kept coming back to it. I kept saying, "If I were a movie director, would I do it or not?" I couldn't answer it for myself.

When I went to see this picture I went to see it, as I say, with a sense almost of reluctance, because I didn't know if I necessarily wanted to start contemplating this problem at this moment.

Q. You stated that the danger in portraying sexual intercourse and other sexual acts in movies is that the art might become more important than the sexual act, is that right?

A. Yes. I have many conservative opinions, and one of them is the sexual act must be protected.

Q. Is it your conclusion that in *I Am Curious* the sexual act was more important than art?

A. Well, because it was a work of art I think something happened. You see, the sexual act is more important than art, in my opinion, but it is not necessarily more important than works of art, because works of art are also mysteries. In other words, when I call something a work of art I mean it leaves me with the same sense of mystery, of a divine presence, that the sexual act gives to some and that a religious worship in a church will give to others.

Q. Let's take a scene such as the scene of intercourse on the balustrade. Do you recall that scene?

A. Yes, I do.

Q. Is that a scene in which the sex act is more important than art? . . .

A. I would say it was not more important than art, no.

Q. It was not?

A. No, the problem didn't even come up for me. I didn't even see it as a sexual act. I saw it as a parody of it at that point.

Q. The scene when the male lead took the rifle away

from the female lead and threw her to the ground, and the scene that followed, was that a scene in which the sex act was more important than art?

A. That was the moment at which I decided this might be a great picture.

THE COURT: No, the question was, in your opinion was that sex scene more important than art?

A. No, because at that moment the two came together, your Honor, in my mind. In other words, I said to myself, "This is a sexual scene of the sort I have been posing as a problem, and it is also a moment of art; the two have come together; it is a magnificent moment." And I thought it was a magnificent moment because I thought there was a deep, profound, human truth in it I had never glimpsed before, and it seemed to me it had the power of a moment that you have when you have a moment of power in great art.

MR. SCHILLING: No further questions, your Honor. . . .